Modern Peacemakers

Henry Kissinger

Ending the Vietnam War

MODERN PEACEMAKERS

Kofi Annan: Guiding the United Nations

Mairead Corrigan and Betty Williams: Partners for Peace in Northern Ireland

Henry Kissinger: Ending the Vietnam War

Nelson Mandela: Ending Apartheid in South Africa

Desmond Tutu: Fighting Apartheid

Elie Wiesel: Messenger for Peace

Modern Peacemakers

Henry Kissinger

Ending the Vietnam War

Heather Lehr Wagner

CHELSEA HOUSE
PUBLISHERS

An imprint of Infobase Publishing

Henry Kissinger

Copyright © 2007 by Infobase Publishing

Chelsea House
An imprint of Infobase Publishing
132 West 31st Street
New York NY 10001

Library of Congress Cataloging-in-Publication Data

Wagner, Heather Lehr.
  Henry Kissinger : ending the Vietnam War / Heather Lehr Wagner.
    p. cm. — (Modern peacemakers)
  Includes bibliographical references and index.
  ISBN 0-7910-9222-4 (hardcover)
  1. Kissinger, Henry, 1923—Juvenile literature. 2. Statesmen—United States—Biography—Juvenile literature. 3. United States—Foreign relations—1969–1974—Juvenile literature. 4. United States—Foreign relations—1974–1977—Juvenile literature. 5. Vietnam War, 1961–1975—Diplomatic history—Juvenile literature. I. Title.
  E840.8.K58W34 2006
  327.730092—dc22   2006020454

Text design by Annie O'Donnell
Cover design by Takeshi Takahashi

Printed in the United States of America

Bang FOF 10 9 8 7 6 5 4 3 2 1

This book is printed on acid-free paper.

TABLE OF CONTENTS

1　An Honorable Peace　　　　　　　1

2　A Boy in Nazi Germany　　　　　11

3　American Citizen　　　　　　　　23

4　The Professor Enters Politics　　40

5　National Security Advisor　　　　52

6　Vietnamization　　　　　　　　　62

7　Secretary of State　　　　　　　78

　Appendix　　　　　　　　　　　　96

　Chronology　　　　　　　　　　　98

　Notes　　　　　　　　　　　　　101

　Bibliography　　　　　　　　　　103

　Further Reading　　　　　　　　104

　Index　　　　　　　　　　　　　106

CHAPTER 1

An Honorable Peace

Late in the afternoon of August 4, 1969, Henry Kissinger, the national security advisor to the president of the United States, left the American Embassy in Paris, apparently to do some sightseeing. Kissinger had spent several days accompanying President Richard Nixon on a trip around the world, visiting Southeast Asia, India, Pakistan, and Romania. Kissinger had then traveled on to Paris while the president returned to America.

The official reason for Kissinger's stop in Paris was to brief French President Georges Pompidou on the international trip he and President Nixon had undertaken. There was another, secret reason for Kissinger's stop in Paris, however. On that August afternoon, Kissinger left the embassy accompanied by one of his aides, Anthony Lake, and the military attaché in Paris, General Vernon Walters. Walters spoke nine languages fluently and was trusted by both Nixon and Kissinger.

The three men went to the apartment of Jean Sainteny, a friend of Kissinger's whom he had visited on previous trips to France. Sainteny had served as the French delegate-general in Hanoi, the city then serving as the base of power for the Communist regime in North Vietnam.

Kissinger's visit was neither a sightseeing trip nor a social call. At Sainteny's apartment, a secret meeting had been arranged between National Security Advisor Kissinger and representatives from North Vietnam, designed to bring an end to the Vietnam War.

The conflict in Vietnam had begun in the 1950s in the land then known as the French colony of Indochina. A Vietnamese struggle against the French had sparked a civil war. A cease-fire had temporarily divided the country into northern and southern regions. The north did not accept this division, viewing it as an arbitrary border imposed by outside forces. Supported by allies in the Soviet Union, the Communist regime in North Vietnam began sending troops south.

At the time, the United States was deeply concerned about the potential spread of communism and about the growing influence of the Soviet Union. American forces were sent in to South Vietnam, first as "advisors" and later to form a military presence, under President Lyndon Johnson. By the time Nixon, Johnson's successor, and Kissinger took office in January 1969, more than half a million American troops were in Vietnam, and there was no plan to reduce that number in the near future. About 200 Americans were dying in the war every week.[1] More than 31,000 Americans had died since the war began.[2]

Kissinger had spent several years analyzing the situation in Vietnam. In October 1965, he had visited the region as a consultant at the request of the U.S. ambassador to South Vietnam, Henry Cabot Lodge. There, he spent two weeks meeting with political, military, and religious leaders, as well as students. He was troubled by the evident lack of planning for the future. In his diary he wrote, "No one could really explain to me how even on the most favorable assumptions . . . the war was going to end."[3]

Kissinger quickly understood that a basic principle was at work in the guerilla warfare being used by North Vietnamese

forces: The guerilla army wins as long as it can keep from los-
ing, whereas the conventional army is bound to lose unless it
wins decisively.[4] The mistake of the American forces, Kissinger
later wrote, was in attempting to fight a conventional war against
guerilla forces, depending on superior firepower, a strategy that
could be "turned against them by an enemy who, fighting in his
own country, could exhaust them with his patience and generate
domestic pressures to end the conflict."[5]

Despite this tactical error, Kissinger believed that the United
States could not simply withdraw its troops. In order to main-
tain its power and influence in the world, America could not,
Kissinger stressed, suddenly pull out. In an article in the journal
Foreign Affairs, published shortly after the announcement of his
appointment as national security advisor, Kissinger wrote:

> The commitment of 500,000 Americans has settled the issue
> of the importance of Viet Nam. What is involved now is confi-
> dence in American promises. However fashionable it is to ridi-
> cule the terms "credibility" or "prestige," they are not empty
> phrases; other nations can gear their actions to ours only if
> they can count on our steadiness. . . . In many parts of the
> world—the Middle East, Europe, Latin America, even Japan—
> stability depends on confidence in American promises.[6]

This philosophy of preserving "credibility" had led Kissinger
to the secret meeting in Paris. American troops could not fight
in Vietnam indefinitely. A way had to be found to bring an end
to the conflict.

THE FIRST MEETING

Kissinger had hoped to meet with Le Duc Tho, a key figure in
the North Vietnamese government, but at this first meeting
North Vietnam was represented by Xuan Thuy, a more junior
member of the Hanoi government. In his memoirs, Kissinger

U.S. reinforcements, above, rush across a jungle clearing to join other troops that are fighting from their bunkers nearby, and in the jungle in the background, in Vietnam. This photograph was taken in April 1967, when the United States was already deeply embroiled in the conflict in Vietnam.

dismissed Xuan Thuy as "Tiny, with a Buddha face and a sharp mind, perpetually smiling even when saying the most outrageous things; he had no authority to negotiate. His job was psychological warfare."[7]

General Walters served as Kissinger's interpreter, translating his English into French. Xuan Thuy had also brought an interpreter, who translated the French into Vietnamese. Because of this extensive process, the meeting lasted three and a half hours.

Kissinger and his team arrived 30 minutes early for the meeting. They were greeted by Jean Sainteny, taken into the living room, and shown the refreshments. Sainteny jokingly asked them not to throw his valuable antiques at each other in the event of a disagreement, then left them alone.

Xuan Thuy arrived precisely on time, and the two negotiators sat on sofas facing each other. The Vietnamese representatives were calm and polite. Kissinger opened the meeting by expressing his respect for what the Vietnamese had suffered during the decades of war. He then continued by outlining the concessions he believed that the American side had already made: an announcement that 25,000 American soldiers would be withdrawn from Vietnam, a promise of additional troop withdrawals as part of a process of mutual withdrawals, a halt in bombings, a promise that the North Vietnamese could participate in internationally supervised elections.

Kissinger's goal was to get some response from the North Vietnamese to these actions, and to reach a conclusion to the conflict by November 1. But Xuan Thuy was not impressed by Kissinger's offer. The idea of "mutual withdrawal" from South Vietnam did not make sense to the North Vietnamese—the only outside forces in South Vietnam, in their eyes, were the Americans. Xuan Thuy did not even admit that North Vietnamese troops were in South Vietnam. Instead, he replied with a 45-minute monologue detailing Vietnam's struggle against outside aggressors through the centuries. Always, Vietnam had ultimately won its independence. This time would be no different, he predicted. The Americans would eventually leave.

American negotiations had focused on a separation between the military and political situations in Vietnam. As Xuan Thuy explained, this could not work for the North Vietnamese—the military and political issues were connected and could not be separately negotiated in the peace process. Xuan Thuy's position was that two factors were critical before negotiations could take place: All American and foreign troops must make a full withdrawal, and the American-supported government in South Vietnam must be disbanded and a new coalition government must be put in place, a government that would include members of the Communist Provisional Revolutionary government.

In the years of negotiations that would follow, the representatives from Hanoi would change little from this position. Kissinger would offer alternate promises over the years—from mutual to complete withdrawal, from promising troop reductions to threatening increased bombings. The North Vietnamese never budged. Their public and private statements were always the same.

That meeting on August 4, 1969, did little to alleviate the conflict in Vietnam. Each side essentially restated its official position. The only real concession made was an agreement to consider holding additional meetings. It would not be until February 1970 that a second meeting took place.

On August 11, Communist forces attacked more than 100 towns and military bases in South Vietnam. In September, Kissinger held a meeting with his aides to devise a punishing, severe blow that would break the will of the North Vietnamese. Peace was still far away.

AN IMPERFECT PEACE

The war would drag on for many years, claiming countless Vietnamese and American lives, before Kissinger and his North Vietnamese counterpoint, by then Le Duc Tho, could claim to have a cease-fire treaty in hand. Meeting near Paris in January 1973, the two sides finally reached an agreement.

On October 16, 1973, the Nobel Committee decided to award the Peace Prize to the two men who had negotiated the cease-fire treaty: Le Duc Tho and Henry Kissinger. In the presentation speech, Mrs. Aase Lionaes, chairperson of the Nobel Committee, noted:

> The Nobel Committee of the Norwegian Storting was fully aware that a ceasefire and not a peace agreement was involved. They realized that peace had not yet come to Vietnam, and that the sufferings of the population of Vietnam are not at an end. They were also aware that events in Vietnam may yet endanger the détente [relaxation of international tension] in the world. The ceasefire agreement was only the first but a tremendously important step on the laborious road to full peace in Vietnam.[8]

Above, Henry Kissinger signs the 1973 cease-fire agreement that was meant to bring an end to the Vietnam War. Although all U.S. troops were withdrawn from Vietnam by March 29, 1973, the war continued until 1975, when the South Vietnamese surrendered to the Viet Cong.

The Nobel Prize Committee awarded the 1973 Peace Prize to Kissinger and Le Duc Tho in recognition not of what they had accomplished, but of what they had shown should be accomplished. As Lionaes explained:

> They were awarded the Peace Prize because in the course of their activities they had indicated the road that should be followed. No one could know whether this road would be followed; but they had lit a torch on the long and difficult road to peace among men. They were awarded the Peace Prize because, within the framework of the politically possible, they championed a peace which, though it might not be perfect, was nevertheless a step along this road.[9]

The peace would prove far from perfect. The cease-fire treaty would be violated before the prize was even awarded, prompting two members of the Nobel Committee to resign in protest. Le Duc Tho refused the prize and the accompanying cash award, explaining that "peace has not been established in South Vietnam."[10] Kissinger did not go to Norway to accept

History of the Nobel Peace Prize

Alfred Nobel died on December 10, 1896. His will, written one year earlier, directed that the vast majority of his fortune—estimated at $9 million—was to be used for the establishment and award of annual prizes in five categories: literature, medicine or physiology, chemistry, physics, and for the person who has done the most to work "for the peace and brotherhood of men."

Ever since, people have marveled at the incongruity between the man, his career, and the award that was named for him. Alfred Nobel was a Swede who spent many years living in other nations; he spent a lot of time in Paris; and he died in Italy. He made his fortune in his 30s by perfecting the manufacture of explosives, which he patented in 1867, leading to the creation of dynamite.

The first Nobel Peace Prize was awarded in 1901 to Henry Dunant, founder of the Red Cross, and Frédéric Passy, an international pacifist. Nobel specified that the Peace Prize, unlike the other Nobel Prizes (which were to be awarded by Swedish committees), would be awarded by a committee of five people elected by the Norwegian Parliament.

The prize is often awarded to a single person, but more than one person may be chosen (as in the first prize in 1901), or an organization may be the recipient of a particular year's Peace Prize. The first was the Institute for International Law, honored in 1904 for its efforts to formulate the general principles that would form the science of international law. The International Committee of the Red Cross has received the prize twice—in 1917 and 1944—for its efforts to promote international solidarity and brotherhood in the midst of war. The Office of the United Nations High Commissioner for Refugees received the prize in 1954; other organizations to receive the prize include the

the prize but sent the American ambassador to Norway to accept the award on his behalf. He donated the prize money to set up a scholarship fund for the children of servicemen killed in Vietnam.

In April 1975, the South Vietnamese city of Saigon fell to Communist forces. American troops did not intervene. Helicopters

United Nations Children's Fund (UNICEF) in 1965, the United Nations Peacekeeping Forces (1988), International Physicians for the Prevention of Nuclear War (1985), Médécins sans Frontières (Doctors Without Borders) in 1999, and the International Atomic Energy Agency and its Director General—Mohamed ElBaradei—in 2005.

Over the years, the award has highlighted the achievements of men and women from many different nations who represent widely varying backgrounds and experiences. An examination of recipients provides an interesting study of changing global events and issues of international concern for more than a century. As of 2005, only 12 women had received the Nobel Prize: Bertha von Suttner (1905), Jane Addams (1931), Emily Greene Balch (1946), Betty Williams and Mairead Corrigan (1976), Mother Theresa (1979), Alva Myrdal (1982), Aung San Suu Kyi (1991), Rigoberta Menchú Tum (1992), Jody Williams (1997), Shirin Ebadi (2003), and Wangari Maathi (2004).

The choices have often proved controversial, including the joint awarding of the Peace Prize in 1973 to Henry Kissinger and Le Duc Tho for their efforts to negotiate a treaty to end to the conflict in Vietnam, efforts which ultimately failed to lead to peace. Awards were given in 1979 and 1993 to men attempting to negotiate peace settlements in the Middle East; sadly their efforts failed to yield a lasting peace.

One of the most curious facts about the Nobel Peace Prize is the list of men and women who failed to win a prize. This list includes one of the people most closely identified with non-violence, Mohandas Gandhi of India. Gandhi never received the Nobel Peace Prize, despite being nominated five times.

evacuated American forces out as the South Vietnamese who had allied with them desperately attempted to climb aboard.

Kissinger's power and prestige would extend beyond the Nobel Prize and the humiliating end to the Vietnam War two years later. He survived the collapse of the Nixon presidency in the scandal of Watergate, going on to serve under Nixon's successor, President Gerald Ford. He would author many books on diplomacy and foreign policy.

The lessons of Vietnam, however, and the futile results of those years of negotiations, continued to haunt Kissinger. In his 1979 memoir, *White House Years*, he wrote, "We had no illusions about Hanoi's long-term goals. Nor did we go through the agony of four years of war and searing negotiations simply to achieve a 'decent interval' for our withdrawal. . . . We sought not an interval before collapse, but lasting peace with honor."[11]

CHAPTER 2

A Boy in Nazi Germany

Late in 1935, Paula Kissinger began to consider the alarming fact that her two teenage sons would have no future if they remained in their native Germany. Paula, her husband, Louis, and their two sons—Heinz (who would later change his name to Henry) and Walter—lived in a Jewish neighborhood in Fürth, a small town in southern Germany, a suburb of the city of Nuremberg. Only a few weeks earlier, on September 4, when the ruling Nazi Party had gathered for its congress in Nuremberg, Adolf Hitler had stood before an overwhelming crowd of 30,000 people and proclaimed that a new age was being born in Germany.

It was this new age that was the cause of concern for Paula Kissinger. At the rally in Nuremberg, new regulations had been announced—regulations that became known as the Nuremberg Laws. The regulations were grouped under two legal measures, one known as the "Law for the Protection of German Blood and German Honor," and the other as the "Reich Citizenship Law." These laws stripped Jewish Germans of their citizenship; from then on, they were to be known as "subjects" rather than "citizens." The

The sign above, posted at the site of the 1936 Olympic Games in Germany, reads "Admission of Jews forbidden." Heinz Kissinger and his family confronted signs like this, which were placed over the entrances of grocery stores, butcher shops, bakeries, dairies, pharmacies, and hotels, on a daily basis.

laws stated that Jews and Aryans (non-Jewish citizens) could not marry, nor could Jews hire female Aryan servants. Jews were not allowed to fly the German flag.

These laws were merely the latest in an ongoing campaign against the Jews that had been underway in Germany for several years. In 1933—the first year that the Nazis seized power in Germany—Jews were banned from holding public office, from working in the civil service, and from holding jobs in farming, teaching, journalism, radio, the movies, or the theater. In 1934,

Jews were no longer allowed to work on the stock exchange. By 1938, they were banned from practicing law, medicine, or engaging in business.

Prejudice was openly on display in many towns, where signs stating "Jews Not Admitted" were placed over the entrances of grocery stores, butcher shops, bakeries, dairies, pharmacies, and hotels.[12] More and more doors were closing to Jews in Germany, and it was this that worried Paula Kissinger. When her husband was forced from his job, shortly after the passage of the Nuremberg Laws, when she was no longer able to swim in the public pool, when non-Jewish friends grew distant and the boys had fewer and fewer friends with whom to play, Paula realized that it was time for desperate measures. She found the address of a cousin who had emigrated to the United States—to a place called Washington Heights on the Upper West Side of Manhattan. She had never met this cousin, but Paula wrote to her, asking if Heinz and Walter could come to the United States and live with her.

A TIME OF CHANGE

Paula's sons, Heinz and Walter, loved to attend soccer matches. They were enthusiastic fans of the Kleeblatt Eleven, the local team from Fürth. League matches, though, like most public gatherings in Germany, were now forbidden to Jews. Although Paula and Louis ordered their sons to obey the law, the boys still frequently snuck off to the stadium to watch matches. At least once they had been caught by a group of young boys and beaten, simply because they were Jewish.

The boys faced more serious obstacles than being unable to safely attend their local team's soccer matches, however. Their father had wanted them to attend the *Gymnasium*, the competitive and challenging state-run school. By the time that Heinz (the older of the two brothers) was old enough to apply, however, Jews were no longer welcome in the public schools. His application was rejected.

Heinz was a talented and serious student. When he was born on May 27, 1923, Heinz Alfred Kissinger joined a Jewish population of Fürth that had shrunk from 7,000 to 3,000 (out of Fürth's total population of 80,000) in little more than half a century.[13] It was an unfortunate time for a Jewish child to be born—that same year, Adolf Hitler began writing *Mein Kampf* (which would be published two years later) and launched his "Beer Hall Putsch," an early attempt to seize power that would be only temporarily unsuccessful. Also in 1923, Julius Streicher began to publish the stridently anti-Semitic weekly *Der Stürmer*, which contained

Law for the Protection of German Blood and German Honor

On September 15, 1935, the Nuremberg Laws became official in Germany; they made life increasingly difficult for the Kissingers and other Jewish families. These regulations included the Reich Citizenship Law, which stated that Jews would no longer be considered citizens. Instead, they would be known as "subjects." The Law for the Protection of German Blood and German Honor was also enacted, parts of which read as follows:

> Entirely convinced that the purity of German blood is essential to the further existence of the German people, and inspired by the uncompromising determination to safeguard the future of the German nation, the Reichstag has unanimously resolved upon the following law, which is promulgated herewith:
>
> Section 1
> 1. Marriages between Jews and citizens of German or kindred blood are forbidden. Marriages concluded in defiance of this law are void, even if, for the purpose of evading this law, they were concluded abroad.
> 2. Proceedings for annulment may be initiated only by the Public Prosecutor. . . .

fantastical, paranoid accounts of Jewish plots, crimes committed by Jews, and racist commentary and illustrations. The newspaper found an audience and its circulation gradually reached 500,000.

When Heinz was about a year old, his brother Walter was born. As they grew, the boys were similar in appearance—both thin with high foreheads, prominent ears, and wiry hair. But they were quite different in personality—Walter was social and gregarious, whereas Heinz was more intellectual and shy.

Heinz loved to play soccer and *völkerball*, a kind of dodgeball in which teams of five throw balls at each other in an effort to

Section 3
Jews will not be permitted to employ female citizens of German or kindred blood as domestic servants.

Section 4
1. Jews are forbidden to display the Reich and national flag or the national colors.
2. On the other hand they are permitted to display the Jewish colors. The exercise of this right is protected by the State.

Section 5
1. A person who acts contrary to the prohibition of Section 1 will be punished with hard labour. . . .
2. A person who acts contrary to the provisions of Sections 3 or 4 will be punished with imprisonment up to a year and with a fine, or with one of these penalties.

Section 6
The Reich Minister of the Interior in agreement with the Deputy Fuhrer and the Reich Minister of Justice will issue the legal and administrative regulations required for the enforcement and supplementing of this law.

Source: "The Nuremberg Race Laws." United States Holocaust Memorial Museum. Available at www.ushmm.org/outreach/nlaw.htm.

hit players on the opposite team. He loved to read, and relatives remembered him as a child who always had a book under his arm.

Heinz's father, Louis, was 35 and his wife, Paula, was 21 when Heinz was born. Louis took great pride in his position as a *Studienrat*, a teacher-advisor at a high school for wealthy young women. Teaching was an important part of the Kissinger family tradition. Louis's father had been a teacher, and his three uncles had been teachers. The teaching profession had been chosen by Louis's grandfather, Abraham Kissinger, who was known for being a deeply religious man. In keeping with Jewish custom, he believed in honoring the Sabbath by ceasing all work before sunset on Fridays, and told his sons all to become teachers so that they could easily obey this dictate.

It was Abraham's father who was the first member of the family to take the name Kissinger. Meyer Kissinger was born in 1767 and, as a young man, spent time in the resort town of Bad Kissingen. When he moved to Rodelsee, he became known as Meyer of Kissingen. In 1817, shortly after a series of laws gave Jews the right to be known by family surnames, he legally adopted the name Meyer Kissinger.

Louis Kissinger came to Fürth to attend its teachers' academy. Because there was a demand in Germany for teachers, Louis was exempt from service during World War I. He was introduced to his future wife, Paula Stern, by the headmaster at the school at which he was first employed. Paula was intelligent, witty, practical, and sensible. They married in 1922, and as a wedding present, Paula's father gave them enough money to purchase a five-room apartment on the second floor of a gabled sandstone building on a cobbled street in Fürth's Jewish neighborhood. It was there that Heinz was born in 1923.

When Heinz was denied admittance to the Gymnasium, he instead enrolled in the *Israelitische Realschule* in Fürth. The curriculum was challenging; it focused on German and Jewish history, literature, and foreign languages. Heinz chose to study English.

A firm focus was placed on religion, and Heinz spent two hours per day studying the Talmud (the Jewish scriptures) and the Bible. When Heinz first enrolled, the school was small and equally divided between boys and girls. As the laws against Jews attending public schools were passed, however, the class sizes increased from about 30 per grade to 50 per class.

After completing his studies in Fürth, Heinz then went to the Jewish seminary in Würzburg, where his grandfather, David Kissinger, had once taught. Heinz lived in a dormitory, studied, and visited his grandfather. There was little point to the studies, however. Heinz had gone there as a way to occupy his time rather than to prepare himself for a specific career, for there were fewer and fewer careers available to young Jewish men.

A DIFFICULT DECISION

By the time of the grand Nazi Party rally in nearby Nuremberg in 1935, signs of anti-Semitism were everywhere. The Jewish cemetery in Fürth was desecrated. Jewish-owned shops were being closed.

When the Nuremberg Laws were passed, Louis Kissinger was deemed "unfit" to teach Germans and forced out of his job. The experience left him humiliated and devastated. He attempted to start a Jewish vocational school in Fürth, where he taught accounting. Like many Jews in Germany, he believed that the anti-Semitism, and the hold of the Nazis on power, was simply a phase, one that would pass. "He was a man of great goodness," his oldest son later said, "in a world where goodness had no meaning."[14]

While Louis Kissinger waited for the anti-Semitism to ease, his wife, Paula, took action. She soon received a response to her request that the boys be allowed to move to the United States. Her cousin had replied that the boys could not come alone. The entire family should emigrate instead.

It was not an easy decision, but Paula Kissinger was convinced that her family must leave Germany. "Our children weren't allowed to play with the others," she said.

Adolf Hitler speaks to the Hitler Youth at the Nuremberg stadium during the annual Nazi Party rally in September 1937. The Nazis' growing influence and presence in Germany and the increasingly hostile climate for Jews caused the Kissingers to leave their homeland for the United States the following year.

They stayed shut up in the garden. . . . The Hitler Youth, which included almost all the children in Fürth, sang in ranks in the street and paraded in uniform, and Henry and his brother would watch them, unable to understand why they didn't have the right to do what others did. . . . The two brothers stuck close together for protection.[15]

Childhood friends of Heinz remembered that sense of fear when they saw groups of non-Jewish youths coming toward them, the constant sense of being denied entrance to places, of being unwanted. There were stories of being attacked for no reason, of hearing anti-Semitic remarks, of being called insulting names while walking down the street. "We couldn't go to the swimming pool, the dances, or the tea room," Werner Gundelfinger recalled. "We couldn't go anywhere without seeing the sign: *Juden Verboten* ["Jews Forbidden"]. These are things that remain in your subconscious."[16]

Paula Kissinger was more social than her husband, and the insults and the pulling away by old friends was very painful for her. More than anything, she worried about her sons. She was also devoted to her father, however, who was dying of cancer. She was his only child, and she did not want to leave him.

She waited two years, but by the spring of 1938 the anti-Semitism was growing worse. Heinz was 15, and Walter was 14. There was no point in their preparing for careers they could not practice. It was increasingly dangerous for them to simply walk down the street. Many of their friends had left Germany.

"It was my decision," Paula later said, "and I did it because of the children. I knew there was not a life to be made for them if we stayed."[17] Paula's cousin filed the necessary papers to permit the family to enter the United States, and they received the paperwork that would allow them to leave Germany.

The family went to say good-bye to Paula's ill father. When he was older, Heinz would still recall this moment vividly: "I had never seen my father cry until he said good-bye to my mother's father. That shook me more than anything. I suddenly realized we were involved in some big and irrevocable event. It was the first time I had encountered anything my father couldn't cope with."[18]

On August 20, 1938, the Kissingers sailed for London, where Paula had an aunt. They had been forced to pay a fee to move their possessions out of Germany, but in the end they were allowed to take only a few pieces of furniture and whatever belongings they could fit into a single trunk. They were allowed only to take a very small amount of money. The family stayed in London for two weeks, and then set sail for America.

The future was uncertain, but they were luckier than they realized at the time. Only three months after they left, on November 9, 1938, German mobs launched *Kristallnacht* ("Crystal Night," named for the broken glass that covered the streets). This was a series of attacks on Jewish-owned shops, businesses, homes, and synagogues. Within two days, more than 1,000 synagogues were burned (including the synagogue where the Kissingers had worshipped). Some 7,000 Jewish businesses were destroyed. Dozens of Jewish people were killed, and Jewish homes, schools, and even hospitals were looted while police stood by and did nothing. By November 11, 30,000 German Jewish men had been arrested for the "crime" of being Jewish and were sent to concentration camps. Jewish-owned businesses could no longer open unless they were managed by people who were not Jewish. Curfews were announced, limiting the hours in the day during which Jews could leave their homes.

Of the 3,000 Jews who lived in Fürth in 1933, when Hitler came to power, only 70 remained after the war.[19] At least 13 close relatives of the Kissinger family were sent to the gas chambers or died in concentration camps.

As 15-year-old Heinz Kissinger left for America, he was convinced that he would return to Fürth. He was correct. On December 15, 1975, he did return to Fürth with his parents and brother. By then, he was known as Henry Kissinger, and he had become the U.S. secretary of state. He was in Fürth to receive the Golden Citizen's Medallion, the city's highest award, for his efforts to achieve peace in the world. Kissinger said at that occasion, "I am proud to be here as the secretary of state of perhaps the only country in the world where it is possible for an adopted son to have the opportunity for responsibility and service that I have enjoyed." He continued:

> I am happy to share this occasion with my family, particularly my parents, who have never lost their attachment to this city in which they spent the greater part of their lives. . . . Our generation has witnessed, and has no excuse ever to forget,

Henry Kissinger, hand up, waves to the crowd gathered in his German hometown, Fürth. His parents, Paula and Louis Kissinger, accompanied him on his visit to Fürth in 1975, when he was awarded the Golden Citizen's Medallion. It was the first time Kissinger had returned to the town in 37 years.

the dark force of brutality and raw power at large in the modern world. As I stand here today, suffering is still dominant in many parts of the globe. Of all the species on this planet, man alone has inflicted on himself the great part of his own anguish. Yet our generation more than any other also has the possibility and indeed the imperative of something better. We live in a world of some 150 sovereign nations, in an era of both instant communication and ideological competition and in the shadow of nuclear catastrophe. No longer can we afford to submit to an assumed inevitability of history. Our goal must be peace.[20]

Kissinger alluded only indirectly to the events that had forced his family to flee Germany some 37 years earlier, noting that his receipt of the award was evidence of how "we have overcome an unhappy past."[21]

Louis Kissinger shared his son's focus on the present, not the past. At a lunch with the few friends of his still alive in Fürth, he said, "We forget all the bad memories on this day."[22] Paula Kissinger was not so forgiving, though—nor so willing to forget the events that had forced her family onto a boat to America with little more than pocket change. "I was offended in my heart that day, but said nothing," she later said. "In my heart, I knew they would have burned us with the others if we had stayed."[23]

CHAPTER 3

American Citizen

The Kissingers arrived in America in August 1938. Paula Kissinger's cousin had found them a three-bedroom apartment across the hall from her own, in a six-story brick building in the Washington Heights section of New York City, located at the northern end of Manhattan. The area was home to many Jewish immigrants, not only refugees from Hitler's Germany, but also from Russia and other areas of Europe, and the Kissingers found friends from Nuremberg and Fürth living nearby.

Despite their genial living arrangements, transition to life in America was not easy for the Kissinger family. It is one thing to study English as a second language in school, but it is quite another to be immersed in an environment where English is spoken rapidly, occasionally with slang expressions, and with a multitude of accents.

The transition was particularly difficult for 50-year-old Louis Kissinger. There was no demand for someone with his German teaching credentials; ultimately, he was forced to take a job as a bookkeeper at a factory owned by friends from Germany. Louis was painfully aware of his thick accent and afraid of making a grammatical mistake. As a result, he spoke little.

The more gregarious Paula Kissinger had less trouble; she was able to master enough English to carry on easy conversations, and she soon became the main source of financial support for her family. She worked first for a caterer, helping prepare and serve meals at weddings and bar mitzvahs; later, as she grew more popular and successful, she went into business for herself.

As part of his efforts to adapt to life in America, Heinz Kissinger took the more American name of "Henry." He very quickly became absorbed in baseball, learning the rules and the players and inviting friends to go with him to Yankee Stadium. One friend who arrived from Fürth at about the same time and went with him to Yankee Stadium noted that Kissinger "was the first to find out how to get there and how much it cost, and to understand baseball. A couple of weeks after he went to the stadium the first time, he got my uncle and me to go. Baseball was a sport unknown to us, but he explained the whole game."[24]

In September 1938, Kissinger enrolled in George Washington High School. The school was known for the high standards of its teachers and the high achievement of its students—most of them immigrants and refugees. Kissinger, always a serious student, quickly earned high marks, despite being described in school records as having a "foreign language handicap."[25] Although he quickly mastered the nuances of English, he would retain an accent throughout his life.

In his farewell speech as secretary of state, given in January 1977, Kissinger shared one of the rare glimpses into his first years in America: "When I came here in 1938, I was asked to write an essay at George Washington High School about what it meant to be an American. I wrote that . . . I thought that this was a country where one could walk across the street with one's head erect."[26] This realization had come from an incident Kissinger experienced after only a few months in America. He was walking alone on the street, heading toward an ice-cream parlor, when he noticed a group of boys walking toward him. They were strangers, but he knew that they were not Jewish. Years of living under the Nazi rule had created an instinctive response in him—to step off the sidewalk and move out of the way, to avoid the inevitable insults or violence. Then Kissinger realized that he was in America—he no longer needed to step aside.

NIGHT SCHOOL

When Paula Kissinger's father died, the family inherited a small sum of money, but finances were still tight: After one year at George Washington High, Kissinger decided to attend night school instead, so that he could work during the day and contribute to his family's finances. He took a job working for a shaving-brush company owned by his mother's cousins, first working in the factory squeezing acid and water out of the brush bristles, and later being promoted to a delivery boy. He kept a book with him at all times, using his free time to read and study.

"There are all these people who say that working my way through high school like that was also a traumatic experience and a great hardship," Kissinger later noted. "But, I tell you, we had a very close family relationship and things did not seem that hard to me. I was not brought up to have a lot of leisure; there was no shame in that."[27]

Kissinger decided to become an accountant, not because he excelled in numbers or because he felt a strong draw to the profession, but simply because he thought he might be able to get a job in the field. He enrolled at the tuition-free City College of New York, which in 1940 had more than 30,000 students, about 75 percent of them Jewish.[28] He continued to work during the days at the brush factory while earning top grades in his college courses.

Kissinger was on his way to a career as an accountant until, at the age of 19, he received a letter that would change his life.

The letter was from the U.S. government, announcing that he had been drafted by the United States Army.

In February 1943, Kissinger boarded a train for Camp Croft in Spartanburg, South Carolina, for basic training. One month later, Henry Kissinger became a citizen of the United States during the army's routine process of naturalizing any recruits who were immigrants.

IN THE ARMY

For the first time, Kissinger found himself truly experiencing the idea of America as a "melting pot." He was no longer surrounded by immigrants, no longer living in a Jewish community. "My infantry division was mainly Wisconsin and Illinois and Indiana boys, real middle Americans," Kissinger said. "I found that I liked these people very much. The significant thing about the army is that it made me feel like an American."[29]

Kissinger used his skills at adapting to adjust to army life. He was quickly pulled out of the general population of draftees, however. His scores on the army's aptitude and IQ tests had qualified him for the Army Specialized Training Program, a special educational program that sent certain soldiers to colleges at government expense. Kissinger was sent to Lafayette College in Easton, Pennsylvania, to study engineering. In the tranquil academic setting of the postcard-perfect campus, Kissinger quickly became known as one of the most brilliant, even in a group of soldiers selected for their intelligence. He took 12 classes, mainly in science or technical subjects, and earned A's in all of them. Easton was about 90 minutes by car from New York, and on the weekends Kissinger would often leave campus and hitchhike home.

After less than a year, however, the army decided to end its Specialized Training Program. American involvement in World War II meant that the army needed soldiers to fight on the front, and Kissinger was reassigned in April 1944 to the 84th

Infantry Division at Camp Claiborne, Louisiana. The transition from Lafayette to Camp Claiborne was a difficult one, and Kissinger struggled to find his place among the 17,000 soldiers. The training was rigorous, and Kissinger was homesick.

One day, after completing a 10-mile hike, Kissinger and the other members of his company were resting at a rifle range when a jeep suddenly appeared. From it stepped a short private wearing a neat uniform and a monocle and carrying a walking stick. The private called out loudly, "Who is in command here?" A lieutenant colonel appeared and identified himself. The private then responded briskly, "Sir, I am sent here by the General to speak to your company about why we are in this war."[30]

The cockiness of this man—and his slight Prussian accent—intrigued Kissinger. The private was a 35-year-old former German named Fritz Kraemer, and this first meeting would mark the beginning of an important friendship for Kissinger. Kraemer proceeded to lecture Kissinger and the others on the evils of Nazism and the importance of the war that the Allies had undertaken. Kissinger was inspired—so inspired, in fact, that he wrote Kraemer a letter, expressing his agreement with Kraemer's speech and offering his help.

The letter impressed Kraemer, and he sought out Kissinger. "After my first twenty minutes with Henry," Kraemer later said:

> I had a most astounding experience. I met a twenty-year-old who as yet knew nothing but understood everything. I said it to myself, of course—not to Henry. That would be tactless. You don't tell a twenty-year-old, "You know nothing." But his qualities were visible from the very beginning. A natural phenomenon. I said to myself, "This is amazing. He is not the usual type. He has a sixth sense of musicality—historical musicality." It was not his knowledge. He was so young. But he had the urgent desire not to understand the superficial thing, but the underlying causes. He wanted to grasp things.[31]

Kramer adopted Kissinger as his protégé and began quietly promoting him to important positions. First, Kissinger was selected as the German-speaking interpreter for the commanding general, General Bolling, when Kissinger's unit was transferred to Europe as the war drew to an end in September 1944.

As a translator, Kissinger was assigned to Division Intelligence first, and then later to the Counterintelligence Corps, which oversaw American occupation of German territory after the war ended. Although Kissinger apparently never fired his rifle in combat, he did demonstrate great courage and nerve

Influences on the Peacemaker

Fritz Kraemer, like Kissinger, was a refugee from Nazi Germany. Born in Essen, Germany, in 1908, he was educated in schools in Berlin and Geneva. He earned doctorates in economics and law—one from Goethe University in Frankfurt and the other from the University of Rome. As the Nazis became more visible, the fearless Kraemer would often challenge them to street fights; as a Lutheran and a patriotic German he held little regard for fascism.

He left Germany in 1933 to work as a legal adviser for the League of Nations in Rome, where he wrote eight books on international law. As the fascists rose to power in Germany and Italy, Kraemer left for the United States in 1939. He was drafted into the U.S. Army in 1943, where he quickly gained a reputation as an eccentric—the same eccentric figure Kissinger would spot one year later, wearing a monocle and carrying a riding crop while delivering loud, German-accented speeches. Kissinger was not the only leader Kraemer would mentor—he would also become an important figure in the lives of General Alexander Haig (who would also serve in the Nixon administration), as well as several other generals and high-ranking figures in the U.S. military.

Kraemer was captured after fighting in the Battle of the Bulge. Somehow, he managed to convince his German captors that an Allied victory was inevitable, and persuaded them to surrender to him. He was awarded a Bronze Star for this accomplishment. During the war, Kraemer became an American citizen.

during the final months of fighting. On one occasion, he volunteered to remain behind with a small force in Marche, Belgium, where German police were still occupying the town. Kissinger knew that if German forces captured him, as a Jew he would immediately be shot, but nonetheless he volunteered to use his German skills to attempt to discover enemy plans.

In March 1945, the 84th Division had moved into Germany and seized the town of Krefeld, on the Rhine River near the border with the Netherlands. Krefeld was in chaos, its population of some 200,000 suffering under the lack of administrative

After the war, Kraemer stayed in Germany for two years, analyzing documents that would be used as evidence in the Nuremburg trials. He then returned to the U.S. and worked at the Pentagon from 1951 until 1978.

While Kissinger would acknowledge Kraemer as someone who greatly influenced his career, the two did not always agree. While Kissinger was serving under Nixon, Kraemer privately and publicly disagreed with his policy of detente, arguing that it did not adequately reflect the evils of communism and fascism. The two did not speak for 28 years. They finally were reconciled in 2002, when Kissinger phoned his mentor.

Kraemer served at the Pentagon until well into his nineties, providing briefings on a wide range of topics, including political developments in Southeast Asia, economic prospects in China, and French views on nuclear weapons. He died in 2003 at the age of 95; Henry Kissinger spoke at his funeral.

In Kraemer's obituary, published in the British newspaper *The Telegraph*, Kissinger described Kraemer as "the greatest single influence of my formative years.... Kraemer's values were absolute. Like the ancient prophets, he made no concessions to human frailty or to historic evolution; he treated intermediate solutions as derogation from eternal principle.... He will remain to me a beacon that, amidst the turmoil of the moment, guides us to the transcendental."

authority from an absence of water, gas, or even trash collection. The Counterintelligence Corps arrived to administer the newly captured city, but no one in the Corps division spoke German. Kraemer was contacted, and he quickly nominated Kissinger. So it was that the 21-year-old private became the administrator of Krefeld.

Within a few days, Kissinger had restored order to Krefeld. He quickly eliminated Nazis from positions of power in the municipal government, and he set up a system of reporting so that those responsible for transportation, for utilities, for water, and trash collection all reported to him. In about a week, Kissinger restored order and rebuilt the city government.

After this success, he was transferred to the Counterintelligence Corps, first as a driver and then as an agent with the rank of sergeant. His first assignment was to find and arrest Nazis and Gestapo agents in the areas the Allies had conquered. He was quite successful, using such tricks as putting up posters offering employment to people with "police experience." For his work, he was awarded a Bronze Star.

AMERICAN COMMANDANT

In May 1945, with the Allied victory over Germany completed, Kissinger decided to return to Fürth, to see what had become of his hometown. He stopped first in Leutershausen, the Bavarian village where his mother's family had lived. He wrote a long letter home, describing for his parents what he found there:

> I stood on the hill and looked down into the valley, into the valley wherein lay buried part of my youth. The trees were still shady, the dairy was still there. We stopped the jeep where the bus had always stopped.
>
> For a fleeting moment I thought I saw a little fat woman with her apron on and a weather-beaten mustached old man [Kissinger's grandfather, who had died of cancer after the Kissingers left Germany, and his wife, who was killed by

Nazis in a concentration camp]. But there was only the street and the tower.

We drove very slowly, past the ghosts of all the men who lived and died in the hatred of the years. I thought of the little boy who had played football in the yard and the old man who used to stand in the window to watch him. All the years came back and for a minute time stood still. It was like when our friends were still alive and we were young.

If we could go back 13 years over the hatred and the intolerance, I would find that it had been a long hard road. It had been covered with humiliation, with disappointment. Thirteen years is a long time to go back to. I thought of the fine old people that had been so kind, of the long walks in the woods, of what was and what might have been. For a minute the valley was alive with the people I used to know. They were all there. Then the illusion faded. . . . I said good-bye to my grandparents.[32]

Kissinger then traveled by jeep on to Fürth. He went into the home where the Kissingers had lived, climbing up to their second-floor apartment and looking out the window at the streets and park where had had once played. He then went to the school where his father had taught, the school that had fired his father because he was Jewish. The school was being used as an administrative building for the town, and German officials now under Allied control were working there. "We walked through the corridors," Kissinger wrote to his parents, "and wherever we went, men stood at attention, and wherever we walked the past followed. 'Why do you inspect the school?' Dr. Hahn asked. 'I am paying a debt to my father.'"[33]

Finally, Kissinger traveled on to Nuremberg. He wrote of this final glimpse of the places he had known as a boy:

The Opera House, the culture house, the railroad station, the post office were all pounded into ruin. We stood on a hill and looked into the valley. The shell of Nuremberg lay before us. . . .

Those who live by the sword shall perish by the sword. There on the hill overlooking Nuremberg I said farewell to my youth.[34]

In June 1945, Kissinger was named commandant of the Counterintelligence Division assigned to provide order and to find and arrest Nazis in the Bergstrasse district of Hesse. It was a powerful position, giving Kissinger absolute authority to arrest anyone he deemed a threat to the peace, but Kissinger refused to abuse his power in any way. When introducing himself to Germans, he used the name "Mr. Henry," later explaining that he wanted a name that sounded more American than Jewish because, "I didn't want the Germans to think the Jews were coming back to take revenge."[35]

Later, as a college student, Kissinger elaborated on his philosophy of avoiding feelings of vengeance, of the skill of mastering personal emotions when dealing with those who might be identified as enemies. In his senior thesis, Kissinger wrote, "Reason teaches him that to respite hatred with kindness, and violence with gentleness increases his power over himself, over the effects of the body and over the environment."[36]

Kissinger won the admiration of Germans for his fairness and for his early efforts at diplomacy. He attended local soccer matches, and had dinner with local officials and the chief of police. His responsibilities placed him in charge of more than 20 German towns, and he was able to ensure that former Nazis were ferreted out, removed from positions of power, and arrested. He remained there for nearly a year, before being reassigned (again, thanks to Fritz Kraemer) to the European Command Intelligence School in Oberammergau, a resort in the Alps near Munich, where he taught Allied military officers how to find Nazis and how to restore order in German towns.

For 10 months, Kissinger lectured the officers, sharing with them the skills he had used to great success in his own administrative efforts. He was discharged from the army in May 1946 and returned to the United States in July 1947. He was 24 years old, and he had decided that he should go to college.

HARVARD STUDENT

It was late in the summer when Kissinger sent in his college applications, and most schools had already accepted students for the fall term. Harvard University's president had encouraged his school to make a special effort to accommodate returning veterans, however, so Kissinger's application was accepted and he was granted a scholarship.

Kissinger began classes at Harvard in the fall of 1947, joining a university where 75 percent of its students were veterans.[37] After taking an introductory course in government his first semester, Kissinger eventually decided to major in government, developing the philosophy that would mark much of his public service: *realpolitik*, the idea that politics was shaped by practical, rather than moral or ideological concerns, and that diplomacy must focus on the realities of power and force.

While in college, Kissinger dated Ann Fleischer, a girlfriend from high school with whom he had kept in touch while he was in the army. During his second year of college, they decided to get married. The ceremony took place on February 6, 1949, in Kissinger's parents' apartment in Washington Heights. It was a small wedding, with only 12 guests, and after the ceremony the group celebrated with dinner at a nearby restaurant. The couple rented a small apartment near Harvard, in Arlington Heights, and Ann worked as a bookkeeper at a furniture store while her husband attended classes.

Kissinger earned his undergraduate degree in three years, after submitting an undergraduate thesis in 1950 titled "The Meaning of History—Reflections on Spengler, Toynbee, and Kant." The thesis was ambitious, both in topic and in length— some 383 pages, longer than any undergraduate thesis ever

This photograph, from 1942, shows the Harvard University crew team rowing in practice on the Charles River, with the university in the background. Henry Kissinger would matriculate at Harvard five years later, after being discharged from the army. In 1947, 75 percent of Harvard's students were veterans.

submitted at Harvard, and in fact, longer than any that would follow. It was so large that the university created a new policy, limiting future undergraduate theses to fewer than 150 pages. Kissinger graduated summa cum laude (with highest honors), and was awarded a scholarship to pursue a graduate degree.

Kissinger continued his graduate studies at Harvard, pursuing a Ph.D. in government. His plan for his doctoral dissertation was to write a trilogy that would cover the period of peace in Europe lasting from the Congress of Vienna in 1814–1815 to the beginning of World War I in 1914. In the end, however, only the first installment of the trilogy was written, focusing on the period between 1812 and 1822 and titled "A World Restored: Castlereagh, Metternich, and the Restoration of Peace, 1812–1822."

As Kissinger worked on his dissertation, he was given a critical assignment by his faculty advisor, William Elliott. Elliott was organizing a program for Harvard's summer school in 1951 that would bring an international group of successful young men and women to Harvard for the summer—men and women who worked in journalism, in the civil service, or in politics. Elliott enlisted Kissinger's help in what would become the Harvard International Seminar. Kissinger personally chose the participants, adding writers and poets to the mix. He invited well-known professors to lecture the students—people like Eleanor Roosevelt, sociologist David Riesman, and labor leader Walter Reuther. The program offered not only classes in politics and the humanities but also trips to baseball games, the beach, and cultural activities.

Kissinger developed extraordinary skills during this time, both at building contacts with important names who were invited to lecture and at raising funds to support the seminar. The program was a great success and would ultimately last until 1969. Many of those who attended would become prominent and powerful men and women, who would ultimately prove tremendously useful contacts for Kissinger, including Valery Giscard d'Estaing (who would serve as president of France from 1974 to 1981), Yasuhiro Nakasone (prime minister of Japan from 1982 to 1987), and Bülent Ecevit (who served several terms as prime minister of Turkey during the period of 1972 to 2002).

In 1952, Kissinger also became editor of the journal *Confluence*, a small, quarterly magazine focusing on foreign affairs. He raised funds for the journal, invited prominent intellectuals to contribute articles, and so continued his process of forming connections with influential political figures.

Kissinger earned his Ph.D. in May 1954. His dissertation, despite the fact that it had been shortened from his original plans for a trilogy, was well received—so well received, in fact, that it would be published by Houghton Mifflin three years later under the title *A World Restored*.

In its opening pages, the work outlines some of the philosophies that would shape Kissinger's own efforts at diplomacy:

> Whenever peace—conceived as the avoidance of war—has been the primary objective of a power or a group of powers, the international system has been at the mercy of the most ruthless member of the international community. Whenever the international order has acknowledged that certain principles could not be compromised even for the sake of peace, stability based on an equilibrium of forces was at least conceivable. . . .
>
> It is a mistake to assume that diplomacy can always settle international disputes if there is "good faith" and

A World Restored

Kissinger's first published work, *A World Restored*, based on his doctoral dissertation, offers interesting glimpses into the political philosophy he developed at Harvard that would shape his efforts at diplomacy. In the book's final chapter, "The Nature of Statesmanship," Kissinger outlines the role statesmen play in history:

> The statesman is therefore like one of the heroes in classical drama who has had a vision of the future but who cannot transmit it directly to his fellow-men and who cannot validate its "truth." Nations learn only by experience; they "know" only when it is too late to act. But statesmen must act as if their intuition were already experience, as if their aspiration were truth. It is for this reason that statesmen often share the fate of prophets, that they are without honour in their own country, that they always have a difficult task in legitimizing their programmes domestically, and that their greatness is usually apparent only in retrospect when their intuition has become

"willingness to come to an agreement." For in a revolutionary international order, each power will seem to its opponent to lack precisely these qualities. Diplomats can still meet but they cannot persuade, for they have ceased to speak the same language. In the absence of an agreement on what constitutes a reasonable demand, diplomatic conferences are occupied with sterile repetitions of basic positions and accusations of bad faith, or allegations of "unreasonableness" and "subversion." They become elaborate stage plays which attempt to attach as yet uncommitted powers to one of the opposing systems.

For powers long accustomed to tranquility and without experience with disaster, this is a hard lesson to come by. Lulled by a period of stability which had seemed permanent, they find it nearly impossible to take at face value the assertion of the revolutionary power that it means to smash the

experience. The statesman must therefore be an educator; he must bridge the gap between a people's experience and his vision, between a nation's tradition and its future. In this task his possibilities are limited. A statesman who too far outruns the experience of his people will fail in achieving a domestic consensus, however wise his policies. . . . A statesman who limits his policy to the experience of his people will doom himself to sterility. . . .

It is for this reason that most great statesmen have been either representatives of essentially conservative social structures or revolutionaries: The conservative is effective because of his understanding of the experience of his people and of the essence of a continuing relationships, which is the key to a stable international organization. And the revolutionary, because he transcends experience and identifies the just with the possible.*

---

* Henry A. Kissinger, *A World Restored.* New York: Grosset & Dunlap, 1964, p. 329.

Dr. Henry Kissinger is pictured above, during an appearance on CBS's show *Face the Nation* in July 1958, just four years after he received his Ph.D. from Harvard. His doctoral dissertation covering the restoration of peace in Europe during the period of 1812–1822 was published in 1957.

existing framework. The defenders of the status quo there-fore tend to begin by treating the revolutionary power as if its protestations were merely tactical. . . . Those who warn against the danger in time are considered alarmists; those who counsel adaptation to circumstance are considered balanced and sane, for they have all the good "reasons" on their side: the arguments accepted as valid in the existing framework. "Appeasement," where it is not a device to gain time, is the result of an inability to come to grips with a policy of unlimited objectives.

But it is the essence of a revolutionary power that it possesses the courage of its convictions, that it is willing, indeed eager, to push its principles to their ultimate conclusion. Whatever else a revolutionary power may achieve therefore, it tends to erode, if not the legitimacy of the international order, at least the restraint with which such an order operates. The characteristic of a stable order is its spontaneity; the essence of a revolutionary situation is its self-consciousness.[38]

CHAPTER 4

The Professor Enters Politics

After earning his Ph.D., Kissinger became an instructor at Harvard. In April 1955, Kissinger published an article in the prestigious journal *Foreign Affairs* that dismissed the idea of "massive retaliation"—the official policy of President Eisenhower's administration. "Massive retaliation" meant that any conventional or nuclear attack by America's enemies (at the time the greatest threat was considered to be the Soviet Union) would result in a response of overwhelming force from the United States. In his article, Kissinger argued that this type of policy was no longer realistic in light of the Soviet Union's development of nuclear weapons. "As Soviet nuclear strength increases, the number of areas that will seem worth the destruction of New York, Detroit, or Chicago will steadily diminish," Kissinger wrote, arguing instead for the United States to develop the capacity to fight localized "little wars."[39]

The article resulted in a job offer for Kissinger from the Council of Foreign Affairs, the publisher of *Foreign Affairs*. Kissinger was invited to serve as staff director of a new study group being formed by the council to analyze the impact of nuclear weapons on foreign policy. Kissinger accepted the offer and moved to New York.

Kissinger spent the next three years at the council, a period of time that would prove critical for his future career. Once again, he found himself in a position where he was networking with important and influential people, including McGeorge Bundy (who would become an advisor on national security affairs to presidents Kennedy and Johnson), Paul Nitze, and Robert Bowie (director of the Policy Planning Staff at the State Department), David Rockefeller (who would eventually become the head of the Council of Foreign Affairs and of Chase Bank), and General Walter Bedell Smith (former undersecretary of state). He met Nelson Rockefeller, who would become an important patron over the next few years. And he published *Nuclear Weapons and Foreign Policy*, a book written by Kissinger and based on the discussions within the council's nuclear policy group. The book would remain on best-seller lists for four months and shape current thinking about American foreign policy.

With the publication of *Nuclear Weapons and Foreign Policy* in 1957, the 34-year-old Kissinger joined an elite group of leading writers and intellectuals who were deemed "experts" in foreign policy. In the book, Kissinger argued that America's focus should not be simply on developing massive military power, but instead on creating a strategic approach to diplomacy to view not only the risks but also the opportunities of the nuclear age. Kissinger expressed the idea that the United States and the Soviet Union might engage not in an all-out nuclear war, but instead in a "limited" nuclear war: "Limited nuclear war represents our most effective strategy against nuclear powers or against a major power which is capable of substituting manpower for technology."[40] Kissinger's theory focused on the idea of a more flexible response to foreign policy, one that relied on conventional and nonconventional military capabilities as well as a strong nuclear arsenal.

After the book's publication, Kissinger returned to Harvard as a professor. He was granted tenure, promoted to associate professor in 1959, and promoted to full Professor in 1962—a very rapid rise in the academic world. Kissinger had waited until his career seemed secure to have children. In March 1959, Elizabeth Kissinger was born. The Kissingers' son, David, was born two years later.

The Kissingers moved into a larger home and entertained frequently, giving dinner parties for students, faculty members, and even, on occasion, a distinguished business or political figure. One guest included the wealthy Nelson Rockefeller, President Eisenhower's assistant for international affairs. Kissinger did some part-time work for Rockefeller, first as a think-tank coordinator and later as a consultant. As Kissinger's reputation grew, however, his travel increased, and the marriage suffered. The Kissingers separated in late 1962, and they divorced in August 1964.

ARMS CONTROL DEBATE

In the late 1950s and early 1960s, Kissinger became increasingly involved with discussions on arms control and diplomacy. In January 1961, he published *The Necessity for Choice: Prospects of American Foreign Policy*. The book contained similar arguments to those he had published previously in favor of limited war, but in one important respect, Kissinger demonstrated a change in position: He no longer favored using nuclear weapons in a limited war. He wrote:

> Some years ago, this author advocated a nuclear strategy. It seemed then that the most effective deterrent to any substantial Communist aggression was the knowledge that the United States would employ nuclear weapons from the very outset. A nuclear strategy appeared to offer the best prospect of offsetting Sino-Soviet manpower and of using our superior industrial capacity to best advantage. The need for forces

President John F. Kennedy (above) was inaugurated in 1961, around the same time that Kissinger's book, *The Necessity for Choice,* was published. After the book's publication, President Kennedy invited Kissinger to serve as a part-time consultant to his national security assistant.

capable of fighting limited nuclear war still remains. However, several developments have caused a shift in the view about the relative emphasis to be given conventional forces as against nuclear forces.[41]

President John F. Kennedy was inaugurated at about the same time as the publication of *The Necessity for Choice,* and he invited Kissinger to serve as a part-time consultant to his national security assistant, McGeorge Bundy. From 1961 until 1968, Kissinger continued to teach at Harvard while consulting part-time for Kennedy, Lyndon Johnson, and Nelson Rockefeller. During those eight years, he enjoyed only limited influence on policy.

Kissinger was, at the time, registered as a Democrat, and in the 1960 presidential election, he voted for Kennedy over Richard Nixon.[42] As a part-time consultant commuting between Boston and Washington, he was rarely an integral player in debates over foreign policy. In early 1962, he left his consulting position and returned to teach full time at Harvard.

Later, Kissinger would look back with some regret on his abbreviated, limited role in the Kennedy administration:

> I first saw government at a high level in the early 1960s—at a time which is now occasionally debunked as overly brash, excessively optimistic, even somewhat arrogant. Some of these criticisms are justified. But a spirit prevailed then which was quintessentially American: that problems are a challenge, not an alibi; that men are measured not only by their success but also by their striving; that it is better to aim grandly than to wallow in mediocre comfort. Above all, government and opponents thought of themselves in a common enterprise—not in a permanent, irreconcilable contest.[43]

Kissinger continued to publish articles that took an increasingly conservative approach to America's foreign policy. The debate over the use of nuclear weapons was a favorite theme.

LYNDON JOHNSON

In 1964, Kissinger was invited to play a role in the presidential campaign of Nelson Rockefeller, who was challenging Barry Goldwater for the Republican nomination. Kissinger wrote speeches and help developed foreign policy positions for Rockefeller. While serving on the campaign, he met Nancy Sharon Maginnes, a 30-year-old volunteer researcher. The two began a relationship that, although well known to their friends, was conducted largely out of the public eye and would continue for many years.

Rockefeller lost the Republican nomination to Goldwater. In the presidential election, Kissinger cast his vote to reelect the Democratic president, Lyndon Johnson.[44]

In 1965, President Johnson asked the ambassador to South Vietnam, Henry Cabot Lodge, Jr., to seek some fresh opinions on the conflict in Vietnam, which increasingly involved American forces. Lodge knew Kissinger from his involvement with the summer seminars at Harvard and invited him to serve as a consultant. Despite the fact that Kissinger knew little about Vietnam—his focus had been on nuclear policy and on Europe—he agreed to travel to Vietnam in October 1965 to assess what American policy should be in the region.

America's involvement in Vietnam had begun under President Kennedy, when some 16,000 so-called advisors were sent in. President Johnson made the decision to send in American combat forces. During his initial trip to Southeast Asia, Kissinger met with Vietnamese political, military, and religious leaders, as well as students. It was an eye-opening experience. Kissinger quickly realized that there was no military plan in place that could clearly outline a goal for 5 or 10 years into the future, no plan that specified how the war would come to an end. The Vietnamese government that the United States was supporting was incompetent and corrupt, but Kissinger also knew that a withdrawal by U.S. forces would create international distrust in America's credibility. "We are no longer fighting in Vietnam only for the Vietnamese," he wrote after his visit, "we are also fighting for ourselves and for international stability."[45]

Kissinger returned to Vietnam a year later to help set up a program that would inspire high-level defections from the Communist side. Kissinger continued to argue that America's credibility was on the line, that even though a full-scale victory in Vietnam might not be possible, it was important to continue to fight to secure territory and improve America's negotiating position, as well as to avoid what would appear to be a small, weak state defeating the United States.

In 1967, Kissinger's skills were enlisted in a kind of "secret diplomacy" similar to his later duties under President Nixon. In this first mission, code-named "Pennsylvania," messages were exchanged between Hanoi (in North Vietnam) and Washington through Kissinger and two French operatives, one of whom was a friend of Kissinger, the other of whom had connections to Hanoi. The basic goal was to offer a halt in U.S. bombings in exchange for Hanoi's agreement to begin negotiations for a peace treaty. They were unable to reach agreement, and shortly after the secret negotiations collapsed, Johnson ordered an escalation both in the number of American troops being sent to Vietnam and in air strikes.

The North Vietnamese responded by launching the Tet Offensive, in which North Vietnamese and Vietcong troops conducted a major attack against numerous cities and towns in South Vietnam, including the capital, Saigon. American forces were eventually able to fight back and recapture much of the territory, but the offensive prompted many Americans to question statements by the U.S. government and military that the war would end soon. Increasing numbers of Americans would publicly oppose the war, and President Johnson would ultimately decide to withdraw from the 1968 presidential campaign for reelection.

NELSON ROCKEFELLER

In 1968, Nelson Rockefeller decided to once again seek the Republican nomination for president. It was not an easy decision; in fact, Rockefeller at first declared that he would not be a candidate. It was not until April 1968 that he decided to enter the race, well after another Republican candidate, Richard Nixon, had begun lining up support.

The war in Vietnam was a critical issue in the presidential race. Rockefeller's position was not clear-cut; his speeches on the issue (many of them written by Kissinger) emphasized that the goal in Vietnam should not be an American victory but instead the creation of strengthened local governments so that the conflict could be returned to Vietnamese forces. In his speeches, Rockefeller (nudged by Kissinger) also called for the creation of a new policy toward China—a position that Kissinger would later encourage Richard Nixon to adopt.

Rockefeller lost the nomination to Nixon, deeply disappointing Kissinger. Talking to another of Rockefeller's speechwriters, Kissinger said of Nixon, "The man is, of course a disaster. Now the Republican Party is a disaster. Fortunately, he can't be elected—or the whole country would be a disaster."[45] Time apparently mellowed some of Kissinger's disdain for Nixon. Only a few months later, Nixon invited Kissinger to serve as his national security advisor, and Kissinger accepted.

A NEW ROLE

On the morning of December 2, 1968, President-elect Richard Nixon stepped onto the podium of the ballroom at the Pierre Hotel to introduce Kissinger as his choice for special assistant for national security. In private discussions, Nixon had assured Kissinger that he wanted an independent, powerful national security advisor, that he distrusted the CIA and the State Department and envisioned a national security system that could provide a check to these traditional shapers of foreign policy. In his first press conference with Kissinger, however, Nixon essentially dismissed all this, informing the press that Kissinger would serve primarily in a planning function, dealing with long-range, rather than tactical, issues. Nixon also outlined plans to appoint a strong

The secretary of state at the time this photograph was taken, Henry Kissinger is shown here with (from left) Nancy Maginnes, Happy Rockefeller, and U.S. Vice President Nelson Rockefeller. The two couples were on their way to the Royal Yacht Britannia for a dinner with Queen Elizabeth II in July 1976.

secretary of state. Kissinger then spoke, informing the press that he agreed with Nixon's plans and did not intend to assume a public role on foreign policy issues. These statements would soon prove false.

Kissinger set about creating a role for himself that would ensure that he was at the center of foreign policy decision-making. He assembled a strong National Security Council (NSC) staff that would be based in the White House, not at the State Department, thus guaranteeing Kissinger increased access to Nixon. He eliminated the Senior Interdepartmental Group, which had traditionally been headed by the undersecretary of state and had reviewed all proposals before they reached the NSC meeting, and replaced it with a National Security Review Group, which Kissinger himself would chair. In this way, Kissinger would have the power to control the agenda of NSC meetings and all policy papers going to Nixon.

Equally important, Kissinger created a system in which he could order National Security Study Memoranda (NSSM)—extensive studies on foreign policy topics done by the State, Defense, Treasury, and other cabinet departments. Because he was able to order these studies, Kissinger would gain control over what foreign policy issues were being researched. Similarly, by gaining the chairmanship of the review group, Kissinger could ensure that there were few independent attempts to shape foreign policy.

Kissinger presented his plans for revamping the national security role to Nixon before his inauguration. Nixon approved them, effectively granting Kissinger a level of power no previous national security advisor had ever enjoyed.

Part of Kissinger's rise to power was his skill at recognizing Nixon's weaknesses and exploiting them. Nixon distrusted the traditional foreign policy apparatus in government, which had certainly shaped the disastrous position that existed in Vietnam when Nixon took office. Kissinger flattered Nixon. Both men appreciated secrecy in diplomacy and in politics. Nixon hated direct confrontation, and when his new secretary of state, William Rogers, demanded an explanation for the changes in the established foreign policy bureaucracy, Nixon left for Key Biscayne to work on his inaugural speech, later informing his staff that he was implementing Kissinger's plans, and anyone who disagreed should resign.[46]

Richard Milhous Nixon was inaugurated on January 20, 1969. Kissinger, seated on the platform behind the new cabinet officers, observed his new boss with a careful eye:

> He was dressed in a morning coat, his pant legs as always a trifle short. His jaw jutted defiantly and yet he seemed uncertain, as if unsure that he was really there. He exuded at once relief and disbelief. He had arrived at last after the most improbable of

President Richard M. Nixon delivers his second inaugural address, January 20, 1973, saying that the world stood on the threshold of a new era of peace. Although he had opposed Nixon during his presidential campaign, Kissinger accepted his offer to serve as Nixon's national security advisor.

careers and one of the most extraordinary feats of self-discipline in American political history. He seemed exultant, as if he could hardly wait for the ceremony to be over so that he could begin to implement the dream of a lifetime. Yet he also appeared somehow spent, even fragile, like a marathon runner who has exhausted himself in a great race. As ever, it was difficult to tell whether it was the occasion or his previous image of it that Nixon actually enjoyed.[47]

Later, as Nixon and his secretary of state, William Rogers, observed the inaugural parade, Kissinger returned to the White House and immediately set to work, drafting letters from Nixon to various heads of foreign governments. Rather than waiting for the State Department to draft official messages, Nixon and Kissinger had immediately decided to begin the process they would consistently follow—setting up their own "back channels" of communication.

CHAPTER 5

National Security Advisor

Nixon and Kissinger had identified four key foreign policy issues that they intended to address: the war in Vietnam, America's relationship with Communist China, the escalating arms race between the United States and the Soviet Union, and conflict in the Middle East. In Kissinger's view:

> The new Administration confronted a world of turbulence and complexity, which would require of us qualities that had no precedent in American experience. Simultaneously we had to end a war, manage a global rivalry with the Soviet Union in the shadow of nuclear weapons, reinvigorate our alliance with the industrial democracies, and integrate the new nations into a new world equilibrium that would last only if it was compatible with the aspiration of all nations. We had to turn to new tasks of construction even while we had learned the limits of our capacities. We had to find within ourselves the moral stamina to persevere while our society was assailed by doubt.[48]

The conflict in Vietnam was, perhaps, the most pressing problem. When Nixon took office, there were 536,000 American troops in Vietnam, and 200 Americans were dying in the war each week.[49] There was no plan in place to reduce troop levels; in fact, the number of troops was being increased rather than decreased. Kissinger's philosophy, one that he had enunciated many times earlier, was that the focus of America's policy in Vietnam should not be on winning the war, but on preserving credibility for a period of time before gradually withdrawing.

Nixon and Kissinger eventually established a policy that linked the Soviet Union to the conflict in Vietnam. (The Soviet Union had provided weapons and support to the North Vietnamese; the Soviets were supportive of the idea of establishing a Communist regime throughout Vietnam.) The idea was that American policies toward the Soviet Union—trade agreements, arms agreements, and so on—could be linked to negotiations over Vietnam in a way that would expedite an end to the war there. In order for progress to be made in the American—Soviet relationship, specific goals would need to be achieved in Vietnam, and vice versa.

Many experts disagreed with this view, believing that linking the Soviet Union with Vietnam could make it more difficult to reach agreement with Moscow and could block efforts to negotiate an arms control agreement. Among those disagreeing with the "linkage" policy was Secretary of State William Rogers, who felt that the administration's focus should be on negotiating an arms control treaty with the Soviets.

The Soviets' reply to initial discussions was measured. They agreed noncommittally that progress toward peace in Vietnam would improve their relationship with the United States, but little additional progress was made.

TRAVELS ABROAD

Kissinger traveled with Nixon on his first trip abroad after assuming the presidency. On February 23, 1969, one month after

Henry Kissinger is shown above in his White House office during his tenure as national security advisor to President Nixon. In his role as advisor, Kissinger had great influence on U.S. foreign policy for years to come.

his inauguration, Nixon departed from Washington aboard Air Force One for a trip to meet with European leaders. Kissinger noted that Nixon's team handled this first trip as if it were a campaign stop, essentially ignoring the American ambassadors (many of whom were Democratic appointees) and the governments that were hosting the president.

Kissinger wrote in his memoirs of the thrill he experienced on this first trip aboard Air Force One, as the plane touched down at night in Brussels, Belgium:

> As soon as the door of the plane opened, we were bathed
> in the arc lights of television. A red carpet stretched past
> an honor guard. The gentle, sensitive King Baudouin of the

Belgians stood at the foot of the ramp to greet the President, who proclaimed, in his brief arrival statement, that the trip would inaugurate a new search for peace. He quoted Woodrow Wilson, always one of his heroes. There were NATO as well as Belgian dignitaries—technically the visit to Brussels was to call at NATO headquarters—but the Belgians had claimed the evening for themselves and we were driven off to the imposing Royal Palace in the heart of the town. King Baudouin excused himself after some pleasantries, and the President was left with Belgian Prime Minister Gaston Eyskens, Foreign Minister Pierre Harmel, Secretary of State Rogers, and me. The Belgians were puzzled by my presence; their protocol had no provision for Presidential Assistants. My attendance also disturbed the precise numerical balance so dear to the heart of diplomats. Since they did not know how to get rid of me, they added a member of the Prime Minister's office on their side.[50]

This scene gives a glimpse into how quickly Kissinger was establishing himself as a critical player in America's foreign policy. Foreign powers quickly learned that a chair would always need to be provided for Mr. Kissinger.

The trip next took Nixon and his entourage to England, West Germany, Italy, and France. The French president, Charles de Gaulle, had recently suggested that Europe might do better by divesting itself of NATO, with its attendant American influences. The meetings between de Gaulle and Nixon were relatively cordial, although de Gaulle continued to stress his belief that Europe's strength lay not in the strength of NATO, but in the strength and independence of the four nations de Gaulle felt were the key players in Europe—Italy, Germany, Britain, and—not surprisingly—France.

In his memoirs, Kissinger discusses a scene that took place as Nixon's visit to France drew to a close. At the end of a ceremonial dinner, an aide informed Kissinger that de Gaulle wished to see him. De Gaulle, clearly unimpressed by the man he viewed as a mere assistant to President Nixon, abruptly greeted Kissinger with a question: Why didn't America get out of Vietnam? Kissinger noted that the sudden withdrawal might present a "credibility problem." When de Gaulle asked where the credibility problem would be felt, Kissinger mentioned the Middle East. "How very odd," de Gaulle replied. "It is precisely in the Middle East that I thought your enemies had the credibility problem."[51]

CAMBODIA

As Nixon was building bridges with European leaders, the crisis in Southeast Asia was deepening. The leader of Cambodia (a country that bordered Vietnam), Prince Norodom Sihanouk, had ruled his nation since 1941, holding on to power in part by accommodating the demands of the neighboring nation of Vietnam. Cambodia was half the size of Vietnam, and in recent years Prince Sihanouk had retained power by allowing North Vietnamese troops to set up bases along the border between Cambodia and South Vietnam. The United States had bombed North Vietnam but had avoided attacks against the bases in Cambodia.

Shortly after Nixon took office, the North Vietnamese increased their attacks, thereby increasing the number of American casualties. Nixon's team had hoped that the North Vietnamese might seize the opportunity of a new president to pursue negotiations. They were mistaken. Nixon believed that the increased attacks were a personal attack against him, a way to test his resolve and see what his response would be.[52]

Even before he assumed office, Nixon had decided to bring an end to North Vietnamese bases in Cambodia. During the transition period before the inauguration, Nixon had sent Kissinger a note that read: "In making your study of Vietnam I want a precise report on what the enemy has in Cambodia and what, if anything, we are doing to destroy the buildup there. I think a

Above is an undated photograph of Charles de Gaulle, who was a celebrated French general during World War II and went on to become
president of France. De Gaulle seemed unimpressed by Kissinger, whom
he viewed as merely an assistant to the U.S. president.

very definite change of policy toward Cambodia probably should be one of the first orders of business when we get in."[53]

While onboard Air Force One traveling to Brussels, Nixon decided that the United States should begin bombing the North Vietnamese bases in Cambodia. This was a pivotal decision, in part because it represented a resumption of bombing. (Bombing had stopped following a 1968 "understanding" with the North Vietnamese while Johnson was still in office. This understanding was that there would be no further U.S. bombings if the North Vietnamese halted attacks on major cities or across the demilitarized zone between North and South Vietnam.) Equally significant, by bombing Cambodia, the United States would be attacking an independent nation that had not openly declared support for either side in the Vietnamese conflict. The idea of Nixon resuming bombings after only one month in office was a public relations nightmare, and Kissinger advised the president to hold off on initiating the action until a discussion of military options had taken place.

Nixon, then in Brussels with a predetermined agenda, could not attend the meeting without drawing attention to it, so Nixon's chief of staff, H.R. "Bob" Haldeman, attended in his place, together with Kissinger; Kissinger's military assistant, Alexander Haig; and a planning officer from the Pentagon. The four men developed guidelines for the bombing Nixon had requested: It would be limited to within five miles of the frontier, and the bombs would be kept secret, only to be acknowledged if Cambodia protested, at which point the United States would offer to pay compensation to any affected civilians.

Nixon's defense secretary, Melvin Laird, a supporter of troop withdrawals and a frequent squabbler with Kissinger over foreign policy decisions, sent a message informing those at the meeting that he did not support the bombings, principally because the attempt to keep them secret was bound to fail. If the bombings were justified, Laird felt, then they should be able to stand up to public scrutiny. Secretary of State Rogers, when he learned of the plans, also expressed strong opposition.

President Nixon congratulates General Alexander Haig after presenting him with the Distinguished Service Medal. Attending the ceremony were Secretary of State William Rogers (left) and Secretary of Defense Melvin Laird (center), two of Kissinger's rivals in Nixon's administration.

Nixon wavered for several weeks. Then, on March 15, the North Vietnamese attacked Saigon. Kissinger urged Nixon to respond with the planned bombings, supplying him with a memo listing the pros and cons of the attack. Kissinger believed that the greatest risks came from strong Cambodian and Soviet protests, from increased North Vietnamese retaliation, and domestically from public protests and antiwar demonstrations.

What Kissinger had not anticipated was what actually did happen—no reaction whatsoever from the Soviets, from Cambodia, or from the Vietnamese. As a result, the secret bombings would continue for more than a year. A climate of secrecy would sweep over the White House—in an effort to keep the bombings secret, Kissinger, Nixon, and others became paranoid about possible leaks of information. Consequently, after reports appeared in the press about the raids in Cambodia, Kissinger and Nixon began a program to wiretap 13 government officials, including 7 members of Kissinger's own staff, and 4 journalists. The bombings did not prevent the Cambodian bases from operating. The campaign, when exposed, would become a disaster for the Nixon administration.

KISSINGER'S ROLE GROWS

By June of 1969, Nixon was instructing Haldeman to limit the National Security Council meetings to biweekly or monthly. Instead, he preferred to discuss foreign policy matters privately with Kissinger.

Kissinger, for his part, had become adept at flattering Nixon, at predicting what his rivals for foreign policy control (Rogers and Laird) would say, and at providing Nixon with appropriate responses. He doubled the size of the NSC staff and tripled the budget over which he had control.

Perhaps more important, however, Kissinger ensured that foreign policy decisions remained under his direct supervision through his chairmanship of the NSC's Senior Review Group— the group that determined which issues reached the president and when—and through his chairmanship of five additional committees that he established: the Washington Special Action Group, which handled the response to crises and sudden events; the Verification Panel, which managed arms negotiations; the Defense Program Review Committee, which debated funding requests for military programs and weapons; the Vietnam Special Studies Group, which coordinated diplomatic and military policy related to the war in Vietnam; and the 40 Committee, a panel charged with authorizing covert actions by the CIA. Kissinger wrote in his memoirs:

> [T]he true origin of our policymaking procedures lay in Nixon's determination—antedating my appointment—to conduct foreign policy from the White House, his distrusts of

the existing bureaucracy, coupled with the congruence of his philosophy and mine and the relative inexperience of the new Secretary of State. To be sure the organization made White House control easier. It gave me a means to involve myself and my staff in early stages of policy formulation. Though this was not envisioned at the beginning, it also made possible the secret negotiations in which as time went on I was increasingly involved. Nixon and I could use the interdepartmental machinery to educate ourselves by ordering planning papers on negotiations that as far as the bureaucracy was concerned were hypothetical; these studies told us the range of options and what could find support within the government. We were then able to put departmental ideas into practice outside of formal channels.[54]

The negotiations with the Soviets exemplified this idea of "back channels." Kissinger frequently met with the Soviet ambassador to the United States, Anatoly Dobrynin. Kissinger somewhat immodestly reported in his memoirs that for a period of eight years, "the most sensitive business in the U.S.-Soviet relations came to be handled between Dobrynin and me."[55] Kissinger would sometimes determine Soviet response to American policy by offering the casual statement that he was "thinking out loud" and then detail a position previously discussed with Nixon. Dobrynin would respond in kind. It was a way of avoiding inadvertent disagreements or obstacles, as well as major deadlocks. Although Kissinger would meet almost monthly with Dobrynin, conclusive progress was not made until 1971.

CHAPTER 6

Vietnamization

Kissinger had many issues to deal with during these early months in the Nixon administration. A large focus of the public's attention was on Vietnam, however, and it would increasingly occupy the Nixon administration, as well.

During his presidential campaign in 1968, Nixon had suggested that the South Vietnamese needed to be trained to take over the fighting in their country, so that their military presence could increase as the American fighting force decreased. This was a policy supported by Defense Secretary Laird, who labeled it "Vietnamization." It was a policy that Kissinger strongly opposed. Kissinger believed that military force and diplomacy must work together in order to work at all.

Very early in his presidency, in a speech given on June 8, Nixon announced his intention to begin withdrawing American troops from South Vietnam. Kissinger supported the announcement, believing that the decision to pull out 25,000 troops (of the more than 500,000 troops stationed there) would not dramatically impact

Thousands of anti-Vietnam War protestors march along the Avenue of the Americas (Sixth Avenue) in New York City in April 1969. Antiwar protests increased to unprecedented levels as the war continued. When protests began taking place outside his home, Kissinger was forced to move into the White House for a time because of concerns for his safety.

American capabilities in the region. Instead, he believed it would send a signal to Hanoi that the United States was serious about negotiating a settlement to the conflict. He also believed that the action would persuade the North Vietnamese to begin negotiations. In this latter point, he was proved wrong.

As antiwar protests increased around the United States, Kissinger personally felt the power of the opposition to Nixon administration policies. He traveled to Brown University to receive an honorary degree and was deeply embarrassed when more than half of the graduating class turned its back on him. Later, protests outside his apartment would become so intense that he would be forced to move into the White House, sleeping in a small apartment in the basement. By the fall of 1970, he would need Secret Service agents to protect him against threats of kidnapping.

These events contributed to Kissinger's determination to achieve a quick settlement that would end the war. In 1969, as Nixon prepared for a round-the-world trip, Kissinger proposed the plan for the secret negotiations in Paris, in August, between himself and representatives from North Vietnam. The initial talks proved inconclusive, but they marked the start of a series of meetings between Kissinger and representatives from Hanoi that would occur in secret over the next three years.

The negotiations marked an important shift for Kissinger—a shift away from his role as presidential advisor and manager of the NSC. With these meetings, he was becoming a diplomatic force, developing skills that he would use throughout the rest of his service to presidents. Kissinger was instrumental in shaping Nixon's foreign policy, but much of his decision-making depended on the principle of "linkage"—which to Kissinger meant that international relations were nearly always linked to the war in Vietnam. Important negotiations with the Soviets and with China were seen through this prism.

After his August meeting with the North Vietnamese representative, Xuan Thuy, Kissinger attempted to add urgency to the negotiations by implying that the United States would respond by November 1 if there was no progress. November 1 was the anniversary of the date on which President Johnson had halted bombings and a date repeatedly referenced by President Nixon.

As the November deadline approached, Kissinger gathered together a group of aides to debate what might be the response if the November 1 deadline passed without progress. Kissinger believed that a strong military response must be considered, as a way to back up the negotiations and ensure that the United States maintained its credibility. Kissinger envisioned a demonstration of overwhelming force—so overwhelming that it would break the will of the North Vietnamese. The project to determine just what that breaking point might be was given the code name "Duck Hook."

A number of scenarios were debated as part of the Duck Hook project. Several of Kissinger's aides opposed any move that might escalate the war. Thousands of people had marched to Washington to protest the war. Kissinger ultimately decided that it was impossible to devise a single, decisive military strike that would bring the war to a quick end.

"I had great hope for negotiations," he wrote later in his memoirs, "perhaps, as events turned out, more than was warranted. I even thought a tolerable outcome could be achieved within a year. Much of the impetus for negotiations came from me."[56]

RETURN TO PARIS

The negotiations resumed in February 1970, and this time Hanoi sent to the negotiating table a more senior member of its government, Le Duc Tho. Ultimately, three meetings would be held between Tho and Kissinger between February 20 and April 4, 1970, before talks broke off.

Le Duc Tho was initially introduced to Kissinger by Xuan Thuy as his "special advisor." Kissinger was not deceived—he knew that Le Duc Tho actually outranked Xuan Thuy as a much more senior member of the government. Le Duc Tho was gray-haired, dignified, and at each meeting wore a black or brown Mao suit. He had joined the anti-French guerillas in Vietnam when he was only 16; he had spent 10 years of his life in prisons and had fought wars against a succession of foreign powers for 20 years.

At the first meeting, the two sides faced each other while seated in two rows of red easy chairs. Kissinger was accompanied by three aides; the North Vietnamese delegation numbered six.

Kissinger's initial strategy was influenced by a belief that a swift negotiation to the war was still possible. He promised that, once troop withdrawals had been completed, the United States would not leave a small force behind. He offered to allow North

Vietnamese withdrawals from South Vietnam to proceed at a different pace from the American withdrawals, and added that they did not need to be formally announced. He also hinted that America was involved in negotiations with the Soviet Union and China—negotiations that might create a less favorable climate for North Vietnamese interests in the future.

Le Duc Tho was well informed, however; he cited Gallup poll statistics that indicated that support for the war among the American people was slipping. The North Vietnamese leader also noted the problem with the strategy of Vietnamization, the same problem that Kissinger had raised earlier: "Before, there were over a million U.S. and puppet troops, and you failed. How can you succeed when you let the puppet troops do the fighting? Now, with only U.S. support, how can you win?"[57]

The second meeting, held on March 16, was noteworthy only in that the plane on which Kissinger was traveling developed engine trouble and was forced to land in Germany. The French president, George Pompidou, was aware of Kissinger's secret negotiations, and when contacted, sent his personal plane to Frankfurt, Germany, to transport Kissinger to Paris. Once at the meeting, Kissinger offered a detailed plan and schedule for U.S. troop withdrawal. Le Duc Tho insisted that a plan for mutual withdrawal was unacceptable, however. Le Duc Tho instead felt that unilateral withdrawal of American troops must come first, a point he again made at the third meeting on April 4. At this meeting, the North Vietnamese negotiator informed Kissinger that no additional meetings needed to be held until the American position had changed.

Kissinger later acknowledged that the emphasis on secrecy for the negotiations resulted in a "compartmentalization of knowledge."[58] The secretaries of state and defense were not informed of the negotiations until considerably later in the process—in the case of Secretary of State Rogers, not until 1971. The American public believed that their president was being inflexible and refusing to seek a diplomatic solution to the war. Finally, the South

Vietnamese were not involved in the negotiations at all, despite the fact that the fate of their country lay in large part in the hands of the men meeting secretly.

CAMBODIA

In the spring of 1970, the war in Vietnam widened to include Cambodia. American troops invaded the neighboring country, aiming to eliminate North Vietnamese infiltration. The secret bombing campaigns had been unable to bring a halt to incursions from Cambodia; President Nixon was determined to attack what he felt were the headquarters of North Vietnamese military operations.

On May 1, 1970, more than 31,000 American and 43,000 South Vietnamese troops crossed over the border into Cambodia.[59] The public response in America was immediate and outraged. Protests took place in the streets and on college campuses. Tragically, on May 4, a crowd of student demonstrators at Kent State University in Ohio would be shot at by young National Guard soldiers. Four students were killed. Nearly 100,000 protestors marched around the White House on May 8. As images of protests and the invasion of a formerly neutral country further shaped American opposition to the war, the North Vietnamese could understandably feel confident that they would ultimately win.

Kissinger later insisted that the moral question of American troops invading a neutral country should not be the focus of debate. Instead, he felt that the real question was, "whether there were any terms that the United States should insist on for its honor, its world position, and the sacrifices already made, or whether it should collapse its effort immediately and unconditionally."[60]

The result of the American invasion, while having a marginal effect on success or failure in Vietnam, had devastating consequences in Cambodia. North Vietnamese forces spread to more than half the country, and began building up the local Khmer Rouge rebels, a small group in Cambodia that, by 1975, had grown from some 5,000 to a violent fighting force of 70,000 that seized power and proceeded to brutally murder any of the population who opposed them. The population of Cambodia was about 8 million in 1975; by the time the Khmer Rouge were ousted four years later, more than 3 million Cambodians had been murdered in a bloody genocide that turned Cambodia into "killing fields."[61]

Athough neither Kissinger nor Nixon can be held personally responsible for Khmer Rouge violence in Cambodia, it is clear that the decision to invade a previously peaceful nation contributed to the climate that allowed this brutal regime to seize power. In 1975, when called to testify before Congress, Kissinger was forced to concede this point: "Our guilt, responsibility, or whatever you may call it toward the Cambodians is that we conducted our operations in Cambodia primarily to serve our purposes related to Vietnam, and that they have now been left in a very difficult circumstance."[62]

CHINA

Kissinger's strategy with the North Vietnamese shifted during 1971. There were no successful meetings. Instead, the Nixon administration continued its policy of promised troop withdrawals, while forming stronger ties with China and the Soviet Union. Kissinger had hinted to the North Vietnamese during the Paris meetings that these new links would isolate them internationally. His skill at opening discussions with China and easing tensions with the Soviets had won him celebrity as a diplomat and had accomplished multiple goals, including protecting America's credibility as a global superpower. He had created a kind of "triangular diplomacy," playing China and the Soviet Union against each other while extending diplomatic offers to both.

The changing relationship with China would remain one of Kissinger and Nixon's greatest foreign policy initiatives. The plan had evolved from early steps—opening a simple dialogue with Chinese leaders—to something more sophisticated, easing trade and visa restrictions and phasing out or eliminating excessive

Kissinger made a series of secret visits to China in 1971, laying the groundwork for President Nixon's historic visit in February 1972. Nixon, above, was accompanied by his wife during his tour of the Forbidden City in Beijing (then known as Peking).

military operations and drills near the Chinese borders. In 1970 and early 1971, American and Chinese diplomats met to formulate plans for exchanging journalists, students, and scientists. By July 1971, Kissinger himself was traveling to China for secret meetings with Chou En-lai, China's Foreign Minister and Premier.

The meetings were a success, bringing an end to nearly two decades of isolation and tension between the United States and China. Kissinger traveled to China again in October 1971, laying the groundwork for a visit from President Nixon in February 1972. It was a truly revolutionary visit, one that both Kissinger and Nixon could point to with pride in later years: it was the first time an American president visited China, and it came during a period in which the country desperately needed a diplomatic success.

MILITARY SETBACKS

In late March 1972, the North Vietnamese launched a major offensive across the demilitarized zone. North Vietnamese troops headed south into Vietnam, and the South Vietnamese forces struggled to put together a coherent response, calling into question the viability of the "Vietnamization" policy. Nixon responded with sporadic bombings, while continuing to withdraw American forces. The number of American troops in the country had, by now, been reduced to about 45,000, none of them in combat units.[63] There no longer seemed to be a clear link between American withdrawals and North Vietnam's easing of attacks; in fact, precisely the opposite was happening. The city of Quang Tri was captured by North Vietnamese forces, and reports reached Kissinger that the South Vietnamese forces might have lost their will to continue the fight.

In this difficult climate, Kissinger was scheduled to meet in Paris again with Le Duc Tho. Understandably, the North Vietnamese were unwilling to make any concessions, given that their troops were scoring military victories in South Vietnamese territory. There was no interest in discussing a compromise or a ceasefire, and Kissinger broke off the talks.

Kissinger returned to Washington convinced that some firmer American response was needed to the North Vietnamese incursions, but at the same time concerned that an American attack on North Vietnam might force the cancellation of a planned U.S.–Soviet summit. Ultimately, Kissinger and Nixon agreed that a tough military response was needed, or negotiations with the North Vietnamese would never succeed. The decision was made to plant mines in the North Vietnamese harbor of Haiphong and increase bombings of Hanoi.

The policy would ultimately prove successful in forcing North Vietnam back to the negotiating table. The mining of Haiphong halted the North Vietnamese advance by interrupting the supply chain, and it is perhaps equally significant that the Soviets did not cancel their planned summit with the United States after news of the military action was released. North Vietnam had counted on support from its Soviet allies. The fact that the summit was not cancelled indicated to the North Vietnamese that the support might be coming to an end.

It was a success for Kissinger's diplomatic efforts. He had created a triangular balance of power with China and Russia through careful and determined negotiations. North Vietnam no longer could rely on support and supplies from China or the Soviets. South Vietnamese forces still had a numerical advantage in their own territory, particularly when aided by periodic American bombing runs. The idea of a cease-fire had increasing appeal and, in August 1972, after some 12 years of war, the leadership in Hanoi voted to author a negotiated settlement.[64]

Both sides had an incentive to negotiate, and both were willing to compromise. The United States no longer insisted that North Vietnamese troops be withdrawn from South Vietnam. North Vietnam no longer insisted that the current South Vietnamese government be replaced by a "coalition" government. Kissinger also had some time pressure—he wanted to conclude a cease-fire before the presidential election in November. The North Vietnamese supported a fast settlement, believing that Nixon would be reelected and fearing that he might be less willing to negotiate after the election.

The South Vietnamese were not in favor of the changed position, nor did they share Kissinger's urgency for a settlement. South Vietnam's president, Nguyen Van Thieu, did not appreciate the policy of negotiations taking place without him, effectively sidelining him while decisions were made about his country's future. Nor was he in favor of the offer Kissinger had made, allowing North Vietnamese troops to remain in South Vietnam.

BREAKTHROUGH

On October 8, 1972, Kissinger, Le Duc Tho, and their negotiating teams met at a white stucco house in the Paris suburb of

Gif-sur-Yvette. Le Duc Tho had with him two large green folders. Their contents, when read, revealed a dramatic shift in the North Vietnamese position—a shift that moved them much closer to the American position. There would still be modifications needed, but the essence of the peace accord lay in those green folders. The points essentially stated:

Legacy of the Peacemaker

The meetings between Henry Kissinger and Le Duc Tho failed to produce a lasting peace. The awarding of the Nobel Prize to these two negotiators—controversial at the time—proved embarrassingly optimistic. Today, more than three decades after the fall of Saigon, the legacy of Henry Kissinger and Le Duc Tho's efforts can still be seen in the conflict between communism and capitalism that marks life in Vietnam. The date of the fall of Saigon, remembered in the U.S. as the humiliating end to the Vietnam War, is celebrated in Vietnam as a date of victory—independence day for a country that finally freed itself from domination by French and, later, American forces. In the U.S. the conflict is described as the Vietnam War, in Vietnam as the American War.

The city once known as Saigon is now Ho Chi Minh City. Memories of the war still exist, but the majority of the population has been born after the war ended. For them, the conflict is history, and American visitors to the north and south are welcomed.

The legacy of the war exists today most clearly in the economy. The communist government is torn between a desire to build a competitive economy and suspicion of foreign investment. The U.S. maintained a trade embargo against Vietnam for nearly 20 years after the end of the war, in part related to charges that the Vietnamese government—based in Hanoi—was not providing information about missing U.S. soldiers. The embargo was also based on Vietnam's occupation of Cambodia from 1979 to 1989.

1. There would be an immediate cease-fire, without requiring that South Vietnamese President Thieu first step down from power.

2. All American forces would be unilaterally withdrawn from South Vietnam, whereas North Vietnamese forces were implicitly allowed to remain.

Under President Bill Clinton, the trade embargo was lifted in 1994. Full diplomatic relations were established between the U.S. and Vietnam in 1995. It was at this point that U.S. investment in Vietnam began, but trade between the two countries is still small when compared with that between the U.S. and other Asian nations.

The legacy of the war also can be seen in the consequences of the American forces' use of the chemical defoliant Agent Orange during the war—many children born deformed—and the maiming or killing of many who stumble upon unexploded land mines and bombs. The U.S. did offer to send in troops to help with mine clearing, but the offer was refused by a Vietnamese government reluctant to see American soldiers in their country.

But many Vietnamese today are learning English, in part to be more competitive in the global economy. After the war, many Vietnamese fled to the U.S.; there are still many who wish to emigrate to join their relatives.

American tourists are now traveling to Vietnam in record numbers. Some are veterans of the war; others are curious to see in person a country that has reached an important era of transition.

Kissinger's hope in Vietnam was to ensure that America's reputation remained strong, and to prevent communism from spreading. In this, he failed. Vietnam is a Communist nation, and America's retreat after the fall of Saigon would affect its international reputation—and its own military strategy—for many years. While welcoming American tourists, and to a certain extent American investors, the American government is not welcomed with the same open arms.

3. All prisoners of war would be returned.

4. There would be no additional North Vietnamese troop infiltration into the south.

5. The United States could continue to aid the South Vietnamese army, and the North Vietnamese could do the same for the Vietcong.

6. An "Administration of National Concord" would be formed, whose function would be to "organize" elections, making decisions only by consensus and without replacing the authority of the governments in Saigon or Hanoi, each of which would continue to manage the territory it controlled.[65]

Kissinger later noted, "For nearly four years we had longed for this day, yet when it arrived it was less dramatic than we had ever imagined. Peace came in the guise of the droning voice of an elderly revolutionary wrapping the end of a decade of bloodshed into legalistic ambiguity."[66]

Kissinger called for a brief recess, and in the interval, the American team shook hands and with some emotion noted that they believed a breakthrough had finally been reached, a breakthrough that could save the honor of the men who had fought and died in Vietnam. "I have often been asked for my most thrilling moment in public service," Kissinger wrote in his memoirs. He continued:

I have participated in many spectacular events; I have lived with power; I have seen pomp and ceremony. But the moment that moved me most deeply has to be that cool autumn Sunday afternoon while the shadows were falling over the serene French landscape and that large quiet room, hung with abstract paintings, was illuminated only at the green baize table across which the two delegations were facing each other. At last, we thought, there would be an end to the bloodletting in Indochina. We stood on the threshold of what we had so

With President Johnson standing at his side, South Vietnamese President Nguyen Van Thieu speaks to the crowd after his arrival in Honolulu in July 1968. Later, Thieu would express his feelings that the Americans had betrayed him during negotiations with North Vietnam.

long sought, a peace compatible with our honor and our international responsibilities. And we would be able to begin healing the wounds that the war had inflicted on our own society.[67]

The meetings continued over several days. On October 11, after a session that lasted some 16 hours, both sides concluded that a satisfactory agreement had been reached.

Kissinger did not transmit a copy of the peace accord to the South Vietnamese leadership. Instead, he returned to Washington, seeking President Nixon's approval. The president approved the document. It was not until another week had passed that

Kissinger traveled to Saigon to present President Thieu with the details of the peace accord.

HUMILIATION IN SAIGON

In Saigon, Kissinger was kept waiting for 15 minutes, while the press recorded his discomfort, before being granted an audience with President Thieu. What Kissinger did not realize was that Thieu had been given a secret copy of the peace accord hours earlier, and he was furious at learning that, not only had a peace accord been reached, but it specified that North Vietnamese troops would remain in South Vietnam.

When finally ushered into the meeting, Kissinger promptly outlined the points that had been proposed and gave Thieu a copy of the treaty—a copy that was in English. When the president requested a copy in Vietnamese, Kissinger said that he did not have one. Thieu then summoned an aide—his nephew—who proceeded to translate the document line by line.

The South Vietnamese eventually made their objections clear. They did not wish the North Vietnamese to be allowed to remain in control of South Vietnamese territory, nor did they accept the creation of the "Administration of National Concord," fearing that it was merely a different name for an entity intended to form a coalition government that would overthrow Thieu. The text also in one place referred to Vietnam as a single state, rather than two separate countries—North and South Vietnam. The line intended to be the border between the countries was not clear.

Kissinger gradually realized that what he had thought was a conclusive peace accord was not going to be accepted by the South Vietnamese president. In fact, Thieu bitterly stated, "I see that those whom I regard as friends have failed me."[68]

Kissinger returned to Washington. The October peace accord had collapsed, but he gave little evidence of this in press briefings he held in Washington. On October 26, in the White House briefing room, he announced to the press, "Ladies and gentlemen, we have now heard from both Vietnams and it is obvious that the war that has been raging for ten years is drawing to a conclusion. . . . We believe that peace is at hand."[69]

Kissinger was forced to call another Paris meeting with Le Duc Tho in November, after President Nixon had won an overwhelming majority of the vote in the presidential elections. Le Duc Tho was furious, feeling that he had been misled. Kissinger had arrived with additional demands from the South Vietnamese, demands that the North was unwilling to concede.

By December, it became clear that the talks had broken down. President Nixon ordered a series of bombings on Hanoi and other targets in North Vietnam, intended to force the North Vietnamese to concede to the additional demands of the South Vietnamese. It can best be described as a questionable policy—both the North Vietnamese and Americans had essentially agreed to a peace accord. It was the South Vietnamese who were objecting to the terms, but the North Vietnamese who were being bombed because of it. Public protests erupted around the world. The bombing was finally halted on December 30, after North Vietnam had agreed to resume negotiations.

CHAPTER 7

Secretary of State

In January 1973, Kissinger once more met with Le Duc Tho and the members of the North Vietnamese delegation. The agreement they concluded on January 9 differed little from the October accord. The line dividing North and South Vietnam was to remain temporary, rather than a recognized border between the two nations. The differences between the two sides were still so deep that the government in South Vietnam refused to sign a document that mentioned the Communist Provisional Revolutionary government. In his memoirs, Kissinger explained how this was managed:

> Great events rarely have a dramatic conclusion. More frequently, they dissolve into a host of technical details. So it was in Paris in January. . . . The agreement to end the war in Vietnam has the distinction of being the only document with which I am familiar in diplomatic history that does not mention all of the main parties. Nor was it signed on the same page by the parties making peace. The South Vietnamese Communists signed together with Hanoi on one page, Saigon and the United States on another. The

negotiations had begun in 1968 with a haggle over the shape of the table; they ended in 1973 with a haggle, in effect, over the same problem.[70]

The conclusion of the peace treaty contributed to Kissinger's steady rise in celebrity and popularity. Shortly into his second term, however, President Nixon began to be engulfed in the early stages of the scandal that would evolve into Watergate. He was determined to replace some of his close advisors but knew that Kissinger's popularity would be an asset to an administration fighting scandal. After considering other candidates, he ultimately decided to ask Secretary of State Rogers to resign; then, he replaced him with Kissinger. Kissinger also retained his role as national security advisor. The nomination was officially announced by Nixon at a press conference on August 22. Kissinger met with reporters the next day.

"There is no other country in the world in which a man of my background could be considered for an office such as the one for which I have been nominated," Kissinger said, "and that imposes on me a very grave responsibility which I will pursue in the national interest."[71]

At the end of the news conference, a reporter asked, "Do you prefer to be called Mr. Secretary or Dr. Secretary?"

"I don't stand on protocol," Kissinger replied. "If you just call me Excellency, it will be okay."[72]

NOBEL PRIZE

Shortly after becoming secretary of state, Kissinger learned that he and Le Duc Tho had jointly been awarded the Nobel Peace Prize in recognition of their efforts to achieve peace in Vietnam. The cease-fire had collapsed, and some critics suggested that the honor might more accurately be labeled the "Nobel War Prize." Others, using a twist on Nixon's campaign pledge of "peace with honor," suggested that the situation had resulted in "honor without peace."

Kissinger learned of the award on October 16, 1973, during a tense meeting on the Middle East. An Associated Press news bulletin was handed to him containing the announcement that he and Le Duc Tho were the joint recipients of the Nobel Peace Prize. Kissinger had not realized that he was a candidate for the

Watergate

The term *Watergate* is used to refer to a series of scandals that, when they became public, forced the resignation of President Richard Nixon and led to the conviction of 30 public officials. One of these scandals involved a burglary at the luxurious Watergate Hotel in Washington, D.C., where the Democratic Party's National Committee offices were located, on the evening of June 17, 1972.

The five burglars were arrested and eventually linked to the White House, where frantic efforts were underway to cover up any connection between President Nixon and the burglary. Eventually, additional scandals emerged, including government-ordered wiretapping of journalists who were reporting information that the White House did not want revealed, charges of misuse of the FBI and CIA for political purposes, and the firing of special prosecutor Archibald Cox by the president—leading to charges of obstruction of justice. Finally, there was the so-called smoking gun—taped evidence of President Nixon discussing a cover-up only a week after the burglary at the Watergate Hotel—which proved conclusively exactly what the president had known and how deep his involvement in the scandal actually was.

From May 17, 1973, when the Senate Watergate Committee began hearings, until July 27, 1974, when the House Judiciary Committee voted to impeach the president, television cameras broadcast to a transfixed nation the drama of Watergate. Three days after the release of the smoking gun tapes, President Nixon announced his resignation.

Kissinger acknowledged the clumsy mistakes Nixon and his administration made that resulted in Watergate. He included in his memoir *Years of Upheaval,* however, a suggestion that prize. He passed the announcement to colleagues, who offered muted congratulations. Kissinger later noted:

> There is no other comparable honor. A statesman's final test, after all, is whether he has made a contribution to the well-being

the climate in the country was at least partly to blame for the scandal:

> In the early 1970s America needed above all a complex understanding of new realities; instead it was offered simple categories of black and white. It had to improve its sense of history; instead it was told by its critics that all frustrations in the world reflected the evil intent of America's own leaders. The Vietnam debate short-circuited a process of maturing. It represented a flight into nostalgia; it fostered the illusion that what ailed America was a loss of its moral purity and that our difficulties could be set right by a return to simple principles. Whatever our mistakes, our destiny was not that facile. A self-indulgent America opened the floodgates of chaos and exacerbated its internal divisions. . . .
>
> There is no excuse for the extralegal methods that went under the name of Watergate. A President cannot justify his own misdeeds by the excesses of his opponents. It is his obligation to raise sights, to set moral standards, to build bridges to his opponents. Nixon did not rise to this act of grace. But no understanding of the period is possible if one overlooks the viciousness, self-righteousness, and occasional brutality of some of Nixon's enemies.
>
> In truth, the animosities of the President and his opposition fed on each other. And if one lesson of Watergate is the abuse of Presidential power, another is that if a democracy is to function, opposition must be restrained by its own sense of civility and limits, by the abiding values of the nation, and by the knowledge that a blanket assault on institutions and motives can paralyze the nation's capacity to govern itself.*

---

* Henry Kissinger, *Years of Upheaval.* Boston: Little, Brown and Company, 1982, pp. 88–89.

of mankind. And yet I knew that without the ability to enforce the Agreement, the structure of peace for Indochina was unlikely to last. I would have been far happier with recognition for a less precarious achievement. Without false modesty, I am prouder of what I accomplished in the next two years in the Middle East.[73]

Kissinger was invited to Oslo to receive the Nobel gold medal from the Norwegian king, Olav V, on December 10. He was also invited to deliver a Nobel lecture then or within six months after the award's presentation.

In addition to the questionability of receiving a prize for achieving peace in a region that continued to be plagued by war, Kissinger noted that the award placed him in an awkward position in relation to President Nixon. He had been given the award in recognition of an agreement that had been based on Nixon's strategy. Kissinger sought to share the spotlight with the president in his official statement:

Nothing that has happened to me in public life has moved me more than this Award, which represents a recognition of the central purpose of the President's foreign policy which is the achievement of a lasting peace.

I am grateful to the President for having given me this opportunity and also for creating the conditions which made it possible to bring the negotiations on Vietnam to a successful conclusion.

When I shall receive the Award, together with my old colleague in the search for peace in Vietnam, Le Duc Tho, I hope that that occasion will at last mark the end, or symbolize the end, of the anguish and the suffering that Vietnam has meant for so many millions of people around the world—and that both at home and abroad it will mark the beginning of a period of reconciliation. . . .

But beyond all these immediate crises, perhaps the most important goal any Administration can set itself is to work for a

world in which the Award will become irrelevant, because peace
will have become so normal and so much taken for granted that
no awards for it will have to be given.[74]

Le Duc Tho refused the prize and his portion of the prize
money, totaling $130,000, noting that peace had not yet been
achieved in South Vietnam. Two members of the Nobel Committee that picked the prize recipient resigned in protest at the choice
of Le Duc Tho and Kissinger. Sixty Harvard and MIT scholars
signed an official letter of protest, noting that the choice of Kissinger and Le Duc Tho was "more than a person with a normal
sense of justice can take."[75]

Kissinger was flattered, but as the public outcry against the
prize grew, he became increasingly uncomfortable about traveling to Norway to accept the award, concerned about the possibility of public, embarrassing protests. Instead, he asked Thomas
Bryne, the American ambassador to Norway, to accept the award
on his behalf. On December 10, 1973, the ambassador was forced
to slip into the University of Oslo's auditorium through a rear
entrance to avoid snowballs and anti-Kissinger demonstrators
to read Kissinger's acceptance speech to those gathered for the
Nobel ceremony. In it, Kissinger acknowledged that the search for
peace in Vietnam was still ongoing:

> The Nobel Peace Prize is as much an award to a purpose as
> to a person. More than the achievement of peace, it symbol-
> izes the quest for peace. Though I deeply cherish this honor
> in a personal sense, I accept it on behalf of that quest and in
> the light of that grand purpose.
>
> Our experience has taught us to regard peace as a deli-
> cate, ever-fleeting condition, its roots too shallow to bear the
> strain of social and political discontent. We tend to accept the
> lessons of that experience and work toward those solutions
> that at best relieve specific sources of strain, lest our neglect
> allows war to overtake peace.

North Vietnam delegate Le Duc Tho (left) and Henry Kissinger shake hands in Paris in 1973. The two men were jointly awarded the 1973 Nobel Peace Prize for their efforts to bring an end to the war in Vietnam, but Le Duc Tho refused the prize, saying that peace had not yet been achieved in South Vietnam.

To the realist, peace represents a stable arrangement of power; to the idealist, a goal so pre-eminent that it conceals the difficulty of finding the means to its achievement. But in this age of thermonuclear technology, neither view can assure man's preservation. Instead, peace, the ideal, must be practised. A sense of responsibility and accommodation must guide the behavior of all nations. Some common notion of justice can and must be found, for failure to do so will only bring more "just" wars.[76]

The choice of Kissinger and Le Duc Tho would remain perhaps the most controversial choice in the history of the Nobel Peace Prize. Geir Lundestad, secretary of the Norwegian Nobel Committee, later noted:

If the purpose of the Nobel Peace Prize had been to establish peace all over the world, it would clearly have failed. We see at all too frequent intervals how limited the powers are even of the American President, the most powerful man in the world. With that in mind, we can hardly expect the Nobel Peace Prize to play a decisive part in international politics. . . . Some will presumably feel that there is something wrong with a prize which so often proves controversial. A more correct view to take might be that the Peace Prize has its present position partly because the Norwegian Nobel Committee has had the courage to take controversial decisions. . . . Most of us presumably believe that there are many different routes to peace, in which case every different category of prize-winner can have a contribution to make.[77]

Kissinger made the decision to donate his share of the Nobel prize money to set up a scholarship fund for the children of servicemen killed or missing in action in Vietnam. The fund—the Paula and Louis Kissinger Scholarship Fund, named for his parents—was created for this purpose.

Letter to the Nobel Peace Prize Committee

On April 30, 1975, after the fall of Saigon, Kissinger sent a letter to Mrs. Aase Lionaes of the Nobel Peace Prize Committee offering to return his award and the prize money. The letter read:

Dear Mrs. Lionaes:

The award to me in 1973 of the Nobel Peace Prize was one of the proudest moments of my life. Together with millions of others, I hoped that the Paris Agreements would finally bring peace in Indochina. But that was not to be; the peace we sought through negotiations has been overturned by force.

While I am deeply conscious of the honor done me by the Nobel Foundation, I feel honor bound to return the prize. I, therefore, enclose the Nobel Gold Medal and the Nobel Diploma so graciously presented to me in 1973.

As you know, rather than accept the financial award which accompanied the prize, I used the money to endow a fund to provide scholarship assistance to children of American servicemen killed or lost in Indochina. Others have since made additional contributions to the fund, and the first scholarship grants will be announced shortly.

Nevertheless, I feel I must reimburse the Nobel Foundation, or, should the Foundation prefer, make a contribution of like amount to a charity acceptable to the Foundation. I ask that you let me know the wishes of the Foundation in this regard, so that I may comply with them immediately.

I regret, more profoundly than I can ever express, the necessity for this letter. But the anguish and tragedy that have been inflicted upon millions who sought nothing more than the chance to live their own lives leave me no alternative.

Sincerely,

Henry A. Kissinger*

* Henry A. Kissinger, *Years of Upheaval*. Boston: Little, Brown and Company, 1982, pp. 1243–1244.

Two years after Kissinger received the prize for his peace-making efforts in Vietnam, Saigon fell to Communist insurgents. Kissinger then wrote to the Nobel Committee and offered to return his prize and money, an offer that was refused.

SECRETARY OF STATE

Kissinger now found himself in charge of the State Department, a far larger organization than the NSC. Kissinger quickly faced numerous crises. The secret program of wiretapping in the Nixon White House had emerged, and Kissinger was questioned about his awareness of the system. In addition, war erupted in the Middle East in October 1973 between Israel, Egypt, and Syria.

This war would result in a brand of diplomacy Kissinger perfected, known as "shuttle diplomacy." From 1974 to 1976, Kissinger would travel to the Middle East 11 times for negotiations, traveling from Egypt to Israel to Syria, in an effort to bring peace to the region. His goal was not a sweeping peace agreement that would settle questions that had plagued the region for decades; instead, he simply wanted to persuade Israeli forces to withdraw from land they had captured while persuading Egypt and Syria to formally recognize Israel. He used his own skills, forming personal relationships with the leaders of these three nations.

On March 30, 1974, the 50-year-old Kissinger married Nancy Maginnes, the 39-year-old woman he had dated quietly for several years. The couple were married in Washington and had a brief honeymoon in Mexico, accompanied by 12 Secret Service agents, 20 Mexican police, and 40 reporters.[78]

Only a few months later, President Nixon's administration would collapse in the scandal of Watergate. Kissinger was able to retain his reputation, even as other figures in the White House were engulfed by the scandal. In part, this was because Kissinger had spent so much time traveling to the Soviet Union, China, and other countries that he was often demonstrably away from the White House when members of the Nixon team were plotting

Kissinger stands with Egyptian President Anwar Sadat in December 1980, during a visit to Egypt. As secretary of state, Kissinger would travel to the Middle East 11 times from 1974 to 1976 in his efforts to bring peace to the troubled region.

the break-in at the Democratic National Headquarters and the resultant cover-up. As Watergate continued to unfold, Kissinger continued to travel as secretary of state. From October 1973 until August 1974, he visited 28 countries; his travels included six trips to the Middle East.[79]

As the details of the scandal became public, Kissinger realized that Nixon needed to resign. He advised the president of this on August 6, noting that an impeachment trial would cripple the United States and its foreign policy. The following day, Nixon called Kissinger into the Oval Office and told him that he had agreed to resign.

"History will treat you more kindly than your contemporaries have," Kissinger told the president.

"It depends who writes history," Nixon replied.[80]

President Nixon officially announced his decision to resign in a televised broadcast on August 8, 1974. He left Washington the following day.

PRESIDENT FORD

Nixon's successor was his vice president, Gerald Ford. Ford quickly assembled his own administration, but kept Kissinger, whom he knew not only through the White House, but also as far back as the early 1960s. Ford, then a Michigan congressman, had been a guest lecturer at one of Kissinger's Harvard seminars.

"Gerald Rudolph Ford was an uncomplicated man tapped by destiny for some of the most complicated tasks in the nation's history," Kissinger later wrote. He continued:

> The first nonelected President, he was called to heal the nation's wounds after a decade in which the Vietnam War and Watergate had produced the most severe divisions since the Civil War. As different as possible from the driven personalities who typically propel themselves into the highest office, Gerald Ford restored calm and confidence to a nation surfeited with upheavals, overcame a series of international crises, and ushered in a period of renewal for American society.[81]

Kissinger continued to travel tirelessly, but there were several setbacks in his final years as secretary of state. He was unable to conclude a Strategic Arms Treaty (SALT II) with the Soviets, despite numerous attempts. There were setbacks in the Middle East, and in March 1975 the North Vietnamese began an offensive at the same time as the American-backed government in Cambodia was under attack from the Khmer Rouge. In April, Cambodia fell to Khmer Rouge forces, and South Vietnam was

THE WHITE HOUSE
WASHINGTON

August 9, 1974

Dear Mr. Secretary:

I hereby resign the Office of President of the
United States.

Sincerely,

11.35 AM

HK

The Honorable Henry A. Kissinger
The Secretary of State
Washington, D.C. 20520

President Nixon's letter of resignation to Secretary of State Henry Kissinger is displayed above. Nixon resigned in the wake of the Watergate scandal, leaving Kissinger to continue his tenure as secretary under Gerald Ford, who had been Nixon's vice president.

in danger of falling to the Communists. Kissinger urged President Ford to seek additional funding from Congress for aid to the South Vietnamese army, but the request was refused. On April 29, the remaining Americans in Saigon were evacuated as Vietcong troops swept into the city.

In October 1975, in a reshuffling of his cabinet, President Ford retained Kissinger as secretary of state but stripped him of his role as national security advisor, giving that post to Kissinger's deputy, Brent Scowcroft. Disappointed, Kissinger considered resigning, but decided to stay on.

Kissinger's final year as secretary of state found him focusing on events in Angola and South Africa, and continuing to negotiate arms control with the Soviets. President Ford lost his bid for reelection in the November 1976 presidential elections, and Democrat Jimmy Carter became the next president.

On his final day as secretary of state—January 19, 1977—Kissinger gave an interview to three reporters from the *New York Times* in which he reviewed his mixed feelings about the foreign policy he had helped to shape:

> I have to say that I pass on a world that is at peace, more at peace than in any previous transition, in which, in addition, in every problem area solutions can be foreseen even if they have not been fully achieved and the framework for solutions exist, in which the agenda of most international negotiations was put forward by the United States. Therefore it cannot be entirely by an accident and it cannot be a series of tactical improvisations.[82]

PRIVATE CITIZEN

Kissinger and his wife moved to New York. He began an international consulting business, while also working as a part-time professor at Georgetown University and giving several speeches a year. He also began writing his memoirs, as well as newspaper columns, magazine articles, and analyses of diplomacy and foreign affairs.

In 1983, President Ronald Reagan appointed Kissinger to head a bipartisan commission on Central America. For six days, Kissinger and the other members of the commission made a tour of six

Kissinger converses with President Ford on the grounds of the White House in August 1974. Later, Kissinger was to describe Ford as "an uncomplicated man tapped by destiny for some of the most complicated tasks in the nation's history."

Central American nations, producing a report that suggested that the region was a battlefield in the ongoing struggle between East and West, calling for an increase in military and humanitarian aid to the region, and specifically citing human rights abuses by death squads in El Salvador.

On several occasions, Kissinger considered entering politics as a candidate—as a possible senator from New York, then as governor. In the end, these ideas never came to fruition.

Most recently, Kissinger has served as an international consultant with his firm, Kissinger Associates. The firm began active operation in July 1982 and enables Kissinger to share his foreign policy and diplomatic skills with private corporations. The clients he gathered for Kissinger Associates would prove problematic for Kissinger in 2002, when he was asked to chair the commission on the terrorist attacks against the United States on September 11, 2001.

At the age of 79, Kissinger had been named by President George W. Bush to head up the 10-member commission in November 2002. Shortly after the announcement was made, however, questions arose by many who said that Kissinger had a conflict of interest due to his close ties to powerful national and international figures, which would make it difficult for him to provide impartial and fair review of the facts that had led up to the terrorist attacks. Kissinger was forced to step down.

KISSINGER'S LEGACY

As President Nixon was preparing to resign the presidency, Kissinger assured him that history would treat him more kindly than his contemporaries had. It is ironic that Kissinger's experience has, in some sense, been the opposite. Praised and acclaimed during his time as secretary of state, Kissinger has in more recent years become a figure sparking debate and controversy. The controversy began, in a sense, at the time of the awarding of the Nobel Peace Prize and has continued in the ensuing years.

Kissinger's accomplishments are noteworthy, and they are well beyond the scope of a book focusing on his role as a Nobel laureate. He was a principal architect of a policy that created a new era in U.S.–China relations. He propelled U.S.–Soviet relations into a more relaxed climate, and worked tirelessly to achieve a peaceful resolution to conflicts in the Middle East.

However, if Kissinger is to be given credit for successes in relations with China and the Soviet Union, then he must also share the blame for the shameful end of the conflict in Vietnam and Cambodia. He failed to recognize the importance of involving

Mayor Rudolph Guiliani of New York (left) gestures at the damage caused by the terrorist attacks of September 11, 2001, at Ground Zero. The next year, President George W. Bush asked Kissinger to chair a commission investigating the attacks, but Kissinger was forced to step down after only a short time as chair.

local countries in solving regional problems, focusing too intently on a system of triangular diplomacy that saw the world through the prism of U.S.–Chinese–Soviet relations.

It was Kissinger who, in large part, launched American foreign policy into a new era. The fifty-sixth secretary of state oversaw great triumphs during his tenure as America's leading statesman. He also witnessed—and must be held at least partly responsible for—great failures, however.

In 2001, Kissinger noted, "The ultimate dilemma of the statesman is to strike a balance between values and interests and, occasionally, between peace and justice."[83] It is precisely this effort that resulted in Kissinger's receipt of the Nobel Peace Prize, and it is this balance that has made him one of the prize's most controversial recipients.

Henry Kissinger's Nobel Peace Prize Acceptance Speech Delivered on December 10, 1973, by Thomas R. Byrne, Ambassador of the United States to Norway

The Nobel Peace Prize is as much an award to a purpose as to a person. More than the achievement of peace, it symbolizes the quest for peace. Though I deeply cherish this honor in a personal sense, I accept it on behalf of that quest and in the light of that grand purpose.

Our experience has taught us to regard peace as a delicate, ever-fleeting condition, its roots too shallow to bear the strain of social and political discontent. We tend to accept the lessons of that experience and work toward those solutions that at best relieve specific sources of strain, lest our neglect allows war to overtake peace.

To the realist, peace represents a stable arrangement of power; to the idealist, a goal so pre-eminent that it conceals the difficulty of finding the means to its achievement. But in this age of thermonuclear technology, neither view can assure man's preservation. Instead, peace, the ideal, must be practiced. A sense of responsibility and accommodation must guide the behavior of all nations. Some common notion of justice can and must be found, for failure to do so will only bring more "just" wars.

In his Nobel acceptance speech, William Faulkner expressed his hope that "man will not merely endure, he will prevail." We live today in a world so complex that even only to endure, man must prevail—over an accelerating technology that threatens to escape his control and over the habits of conflict that have obscured his peaceful nature.

Certain war has yielded to an uncertain peace in Vietnam. Where there was once only despair and dislocation, today there is hope, however frail. In the Middle East, the resumption of full-scale war haunts a fragile ceasefire. In Indochina, the Middle East, and elsewhere, lasting peace will not have been won until contending nations realize the futility of replacing political competition with armed conflict.

America's goal is the building of a structure of peace, a peace in which all nations have a stake and therefore to which all nations have a commitment. We are seeking a stable world, not as an end in itself but as a bridge to the realization of man's noble aspirations of tranquility and community.

If peace, the ideal, is to be our common destiny, then peace, the experience, must be our common practice. For this to be so, the leaders of all nations must remember that their political decisions of war or peace are realized in the human suffering or well-being of their people.

As Alfred Nobel recognized, peace cannot be achieved by one man or one nation. It results from the efforts of men of broad vision and goodwill throughout the world. The accomplishments of individuals need not be remembered, for if lasting peace is to come, it will be the accomplishment of all mankind.

With these thoughts, I extend to you my most sincere appreciation for this award.

1923 Heinz Alfred (Henry) Kissinger is born on May 27.

1933 Nazis seize power in Germany.

1935 Nuremberg rally is held; Nuremburg Laws are passed.

1938 Kissingers leave Germany for America on August 20.

1943 Kissinger begins basic training; becomes U.S. citizen.

1944 Kissinger's unit is transferred to Europe.

1945 Kissinger becomes administrator of Krefield, Germany; returns to Fürth; is named Commandant of the Counterintelligence Division.

1947 Kissinger returns to U.S.; enrolls in Harvard.

1949 Kissinger marries Ann Fleischer.

1951 Kissinger helps organize Harvard International Seminar.

1952 Kissinger becomes editor of *Confluence*.

1954 Kissinger earns Ph.D.; becomes instructor at Harvard.

1955 Kissinger begins work for Council of Foreign Affairs.

1957 *Nuclear Weapons and Foreign Policy* is published.

1959 Kissinger is promoted to Associate Professor; daughter Elizabeth Kissinger is born.

1961	Son David Kissinger is born; *The Necessity for Choice* is published; Kissinger serves as part-time consultant to McGeorge Bundy.
1962	Kissinger is promoted to full Professor; Henry and Ann Kissinger separate.
1964	Kissingers divorce; Henry Kissinger joins Rockefeller campaign.
1968	Kissinger become Special Assistant for National Security to President Nixon.
1969	Kissinger holds secret negotiations with North Vietnamese in Paris.
1970	Kissinger first meets with Le Duc Tho; war in Vietnam widens to include Cambodia.
1971	Kissinger makes series of secret visits to China.
1972	Nixon makes first American presidential visit to China; Kissinger and Le Duc Tho agree to peace accord.
1973	Kissinger becomes Secretary of State; he and Le Duc Tho are jointly awarded Nobel Peace Prize.
1974	Kissinger begins "shuttle diplomacy" in Middle East; marries Nancy Maginnes; President Nixon resigns.
1975	Saigon falls; Kissinger offers to return Nobel Prize; Kissinger is stripped of role as National Security Advisor by President Ford.
1977	Kissinger leaves office as Secretary of State when Jimmy Carter begins presidency.

1982   Kissinger launches consulting firm, Kissinger Associates.

1983   Kissinger appointed by President Reagan to head bipartisan commission on Central America.

2002   Kissinger asked to head up commission investigating the 9/11 terrorist attacks against the U.S.; quickly forced to step down because of potential conflict of interest.

Chapter 1

1. Walter Isaacson, *Kissinger*. New York: Simon & Schuster, 1992, p. 159.
2. Ibid., p. 158.
3. Ibid., p. 118.
4. Henry Kissinger, *Diplomacy*. New York: Simon & Schuster, 1994, p. 629.
5. Ibid., p. 630.
6. Quoted in Isaacson, *Kissinger*, p. 160.
7. Henry Kissinger, *White House Years*. Boston: Little, Brown, 1979, p. 278.
8. Aase Lionaes. "The Nobel Peace Prize 1973: Presentation Speech." Available at www.nobelprize.org/peace/laureates/1973/press.html.
9. Ibid.
10. Quoted in Isaacson, *Kissinger*, p. 507.
11. Kissinger, *White House Years*, p. 1470.

Chapter 2

12. William L. Shirer, *The Rise and Fall of the Third Reich*. New York: Touchstone Books, 1988, p. 233.
13. Isaacson, *Kissinger*, p. 21.
14. Quoted in Marvin Kalb and Bernard Kalb, *Kissinger*. Boston: Little, Brown, 1974, p. 34.
15. Ibid., p. 35.
16. Quoted in Isaacson, *Kissinger*, p. 27.
17. Ibid.
18. Ibid.
19. Kalb and Kalb, *Kissinger*, p. 35.
20. Dan Synovec. "Henry Kissinger returns to his hometown in Germany." *Stars and Stripes*. December 16, 1975. Available at www.stripes.com.
21. Ibid.
22. Quoted in Isaacson, *Kissinger*, p. 28.
23. Ibid.

Chapter 3

24. Ibid., p. 34.
25. Kalb and Kalb, *Kissinger*, p. 36.
26. Quoted in Isaacson, *Kissinger*, p. 33.
27. Quoted in Kalb and Kalb, *Kissinger*, p. 37.
28. Isaacson, *Kissinger*, p. 38.
29. Ibid., p. 40.
30. Quoted in Kalb and Kalb, *Kissinger*, p. 38.
31. Ibid., p. 39.
32. Isaacson, *Kissinger*, p. 50.
33. Ibid., p. 51.
34. Ibid.
35. Ibid., p. 54.
36. Quoted in Bruce Mazlish, *Kissinger: The European Mind in American Policy*. New York: Basic Books, 1976, p. 45.
37. Isaacson, *Kissinger*, p. 59.
38. Henry A. Kissinger, *A World Restored*. New York: Grosset & Dunlap, 1964, pp. 1–3.

Chapter 4

39. Quoted in Isaacson, *Kissinger*, pp. 82–83.

40. Quoted in Jussi Hanhimäki, *The Flawed Architect: Henry Kissinger and American Foreign Policy.* New York: Oxford University Press, 2004, p. 10.
41. Quoted in Kalb and Kalb, *Kissinger,* p. 60.
42. Isaacson, *Kissinger,* p. 109.
43. Quoted in Kalb and Kalb, *Kissinger,* p. 64.
44. Isaacson, *Kissinger,* p. 116.
45. Ibid., pp. 127–128.
46. Ibid., p. 156.
47. Kissinger, *White House Years*, p. 3.

Chapter 5

48. Ibid., pp. 69–70.
49. Isaacson, *Kissinger,* p. 159.
50. Kissinger, *White House Years,* p. 79.
51. Ibid., p. 110.
52. Isaacson, *Kissinger,* p. 173.
53. Kissinger, *White House Years*, p. 241.
54. Ibid., p. 47.
55. Ibid., p. 138.

Chapter 6

56. Ibid., p. 262.
57. Ibid., p. 444.
58. Ibid., p. 448.
59. Isaacson, *Kissinger,* p. 269.
60. Kissinger, *White House Years*, p. 515.
61. Isaacson, *Kissinger,* p. 274.
62. Ibid., pp. 274–275.
63. Ibid., p. 416.
64. Ibid., p. 440.

65. Ibid., p. 448.
66. Kissinger, *White House Years*, p. 1345.
67. Ibid., pp. 1345–1346.
68. Ibid., p. 1385.
69. Quoted in Kalb and Kalb, *Kissinger,* p. 382.

Chapter 7

70. Kissinger, *White House Years*, pp. 1464–1465.
71. Quoted in Kalb and Kalb, *Kissinger,* p. 447.
72. Ibid.
73. Henry Kissinger, *Years of Upheaval.* Boston: Little, Brown and Company, 1982, p. 370.
74. Ibid., p. 371.
75. Quoted in Isaacson, *Kissinger,* p. 508.
76. Henry Kissinger. "Nobel Peace Prize 1973: Acceptance Speech." Available at www.nobelprize.org/peace/laureates/1973/kissinger-acceptance.html.
77. Geir Lundestad. "Reflections on the Nobel Peace Prize." Available at www.nobelprize.org/peace/articles/lundestad/.
78. Isaacson, *Kissinger,* p. 591.
79. Ibid., p. 595.
80. Quoted in Hanhimäki, *The Flawed Architect,* p. 357.
81. Henry Kissinger, *Years of Renewal.* New York: Simon & Schuster, 1999, p. 17.
82. Quoted in Hanhimäki, *The Flawed Architect,* p. 455.
83. Ibid., p. 489.

Books

Hanhimäki, Jussi. *The Flawed Architect: Henry Kissinger and American Foreign Policy*. New York: Oxford University Press, 2004.

Isaacson, Walter. *Kissinger*. New York: Simon & Schuster, 1992.

Kalb, Marvin, and Bernard Kalb. *Kissinger*. Boston: Little, Brown, 1974.

Kissinger, Henry. *Diplomacy*. New York: Simon & Schuster, 1994.

———. *White House Years*. Boston: Little, Brown, 1979.

———. *A World Restored*. New York: Grosset & Dunlap, 1964.

———. *Years of Renewal*. New York: Simon & Schuster, 1999.

———. *Years of Upheaval*. Boston: Little, Brown, 1982.

Mazlish, Bruce. *Kissinger: The European Mind in American Policy*. New York: Basic Books, 1976.

Shirer, William L. *The Rise and Fall of the Third Reich*. New York: Touchstone Books, 1987.

Web sites

Watergate Facts
www.cnn.com/allpolitics/1997/gen/resources/watergate/

Jewish Virtual Library
www.jewishvirtuallibrary.org/jsource/Holocaust/

Stars & Stripes
www.stripes.com

United States Holocaust Memorial Museum
www.ushmm.org

FURTHER READING

Books

Halberstam, David. *The Best and the Brightest*. New York: Ballantine Books, 1993.

Karnow, Stanley. *Vietnam: A History*. New York: Penguin, 1997.

Kissinger, Henry. *White House Years*. Boston: Little, Brown, 1979.

Nixon, Richard Milhous. *RN: The Memoirs of Richard Nixon*. New York: Grosset & Dunlap, 1978.

Woodward, Bob, and Carl Bernstein. *All the President's Men*. New York: Simon & Schuster, 1994.

Web sites

All Peace Prize Winners
www.nobelprize.org/peace/laureates/

Gerald Rudolph Ford
www.americanpresident.org/history/geraldford/

Henry Kissinger
www.npr.org/programs/npc/2002/020305.hkissinger.html

The Nuremberg Race Laws
www.ushmm.org/outreach/nlaw.htm

Revisiting Watergate
www.washingtonpost.com/wp-srv/national/longterm/watergate/

Vietnam Online
www.pbs.org/wgbh/amex/vietnam/

Watergate.info
www.watergate.info

Watergate: 25th Anniversary
www.cnn.com/ALLPOLITICS/1997/gen/resources/watergate/

PICTURE CREDITS

INDEX

A

account career, plans for, 25–26
Administration of National Concord, 75
Agent Orange, 74–75
Angola, 90
antiwar protests, 63–64
arms control debate, 42–44
Army, 26–30, 31–33
Army Specialized Training Program, 26

B

baseball, 24
Battle of the Bulge, 28
Beer Hall Putsch, 14
Belgium, 29
bombings, 58–60, 76
Bowie, Robert, 41
Bronze Star, 30
Brown University, 63
Bundy, McGeorge, 41, 44
Bush, George W., 93, 94
Byrne, Thomas, 83, 96

C

Cambodia, 56–60, 67–68
Camp Clairborne, 27–28
Carter, Jimmy, 91
China, relationship with, 68–69
Chou En-lai, 69
citizenship, Nuremberg Laws and, 11–12
City College of New York, 25
Clinton, William J., 74
Communism, defections and, 46
Communist Provisional Revolutionary Government, 77
concentration camps, 20
Confluence, 35
consulting business, 91–93
controversy, Nobel Peace Prize and, 8–9, 81–83, 84–85
Council of Foreign Affairs, 41
Counterintelligence Corps, 28–30, 32
Cox, Archibald, 80
credibility, 56
Crystal Night, 20

D

De Gaulle, Charles, 55–56, 57
defections, communist, 46
Defense Program Review Committee, 60
Der Stürmer, 14–15
D'Estaing, Valery Giscard, 35
detente, Fritz Kraemer and, 29
Division Intelligence, 28
Dobrynin, Anatoly, 61
Doctors Without Borders, 9
draft, 26
Duck Hook, 65
Dunant, Henry, 8

E

Ecevit, Bülent, 35
Egypt, conflicts in, 85–87
ElBaradei, Mohammed, 9
Elliott, William, 35
embargo (trade), 74
engineering studies, 26
En-lai, Chou, 69
European Command Intelligence

School, 32–33

F

Fleischer, Ann (wife). See Kissinger, Ann (wife)
Ford, Gerald, 10, 89–91
Foreign Affairs, 40–41
40 Committee, 60
Fürth
    departure from, 17–20
    early life in, 13–17
    return to, 20–21, 30–32

G

Gandhi, Mohandas, 9
genocide in Cambodia, 68
George Washington High School, 24, 25
Georgetown University, 91
Golden Citizen's Medallion, 20–21
Goldwater, Barry, 45
Guiliani, Rudolph, 94
Gymnasium, 13–14, 16

H

Haig, Alexander, 28, 58, 59
Haiphong, mining of, 70–71
Haldeman, H.R., 58
Hanoi, bombing of, 76
Harvard International Seminar, 35
Harvard University, 33–38, 40, 42
Hitler Youth, 18
Ho Chi Minh City, 9–10, 46, 73–76

I

International Atomic Energy Agency, 9
International Committee of the Red Cross, 8
Israel, conflicts in, 87–88
Israelitische Realschule, 16–17

J

Johnson, Lyndon B., 2, 44, 45–46, 75

K

Kennedy, John F., 43, 44
Kent State University, 67
Khmer Rouge, 67–68, 89
Kissinger, Abraham (grandfather), 16
Kissinger, Ann (wife), 33, 42
Kissinger, David (son), 42
Kissinger, Elizabeth (daughter), 42
Kissinger, Louis (father), 11, 16, 17, 21–22, 23–24
Kissinger, Meyer (great-grandfather), 16
Kissinger, Nancy (wife), 45, 48, 87
Kissinger, Paula (mother)
    decision to move to America and, 19
    description of, 16
    Nuremburg Laws and, 11, 17
    return to Fürth by, 21–22
    transition to life in America by, 24
Kissinger, Walter (brother), 11, 15

Kissinger Associates, 92–93
Kraemer, Fritz, 27–29
Krefeld, Germany, 29–30
Kristallnacht, 20

L
Lafayette College, 26
Laird, Melvin, 58, 59, 62
Law for the Protection of Ger-
    man Blood and German Honor,
    11–12, 14–15
Le Duc Tho. See Tho, Le Duc
League of Nations, 28
legacy of Henry Kissinger, 93–95
limited war, 41, 42–44
Lodge, Henry Cabot, Jr., 2, 45

M
Maginnes, Nancy Sharon (wife). See
    Kissinger, Nancy (wife)
Marche, Belgium, 29
marriage, Nuremberg Laws and,
    14–15
massive retaliation policy, 40–41
"Meaning of History- Reflections
    on Spengler, Toynbee, and Kant,
    The," 33–34
Mein Kampf, 14
Middle East, 87–88, 89
mining of Haiphong, 70–71

N
Nakasone, Yashuhiro, 35
National Security Advisor, Vietnam
    and, 1–3

National Security Council, 48, 60,
    80
National Security Review Group,
    49, 60
National Security Study Memo-
    randa, 49
Nazis, 11–13, 32
The Necessity for Choice: Prospects
    of American Foreign Policy,
    42–44
New York City, arrival in, 23–25
Nguyen Van Thieu. See Thieu,
    Nguyen Van
Nitze, Paul, 41
Nixon, Richard Milhous
    China and, 69
    Nobel Peace Prize and, 79–83
    role of Kissinger in national
    security and, 47–51, 52–56,
    58–61
    Vietnamization and, 62–65
    Watergate and, 10, 79, 80, 85,
    87–89
Nobel Peace Prize
    acceptance speech for, 83–85,
    96–97
    controversy and, 8–9, 82–83,
    85–87
    history of, 8–9
    letter to committee and, 86
    winning of, 79–82
nuclear war, limited, 41, 42–44
nuclear weapons, 40–44
Nuclear Weapons and Foreign
    Policy, 41
Nuremberg Laws, 11–12, 14–15
Nuremburg Laws, response of Kiss-

inger family to, 17–20

O

October peace accord, 71–73, 75–76
Olav V, king of Norway, 82

P

Passey, Frédéric, 8
Paula and Louis Kissinger Scholarship Fund, 85, 86
peace, philosophy of, 36–39
peace accords, 71–73, 75–76
Pennsylvania mission, 46
Pompidou, George, 66
prejudice, in Germany, 11–14
protests, antiwar, 63–64

R

Reagan, Ronald, 91
realpolitik, 33
Red Cross, 8
Reich Citizenship Law, 11–12
reimbursement, Nobel Peace Prize and, 86
retaliation, massive, 40–41
Rockefeller, David, 41
Rockefeller, Nelson, 41, 42, 44, 46–47
Rogers, William, 49, 51, 53, 58, 66

S

Sadat, Anwar, 88
Saigon, 9–10, 46, 73–76
Sainteny, Jean, 1–2, 4

scholarship fund, 85, 86
Scowcroft, Brent, 91
Secret Service protection, 64
Secretary of State, 87–89
seminary, 17
Senate Watergate Committee, 80
Senior Interdepartmental Group, 48–49
shaving brush company, 25
Sihanouk, Norodom, 56
Smith, Walter Bedell, 41
soccer, 13, 15–16
Soviet Union
    Anatoly Dobrynin and, 61
    arms control and, 89
    relationship with, 68–69
    Vietnam and, 53, 70–71
statesmanship, theory of, 36–39
Stern, Paula (mother). See Kissinger, Paula (mother)
Strategic Arms Treaty, 89
Streicher, Julius, 14–15
Studienrats, 16
Syria, conflicts in, 87

T

Talmud, study of, 17
teaching profession, 16
terrorism, 93
Tet Offensive, 46
theses, 33–34, 35–39
Thieu, Nguyen Van, 71, 73, 75–76
Tho, Le Duc
    negotiations with, 65–67, 71–73, 74–75, 76
    Nobel Peace Prize and, 6–10, 79–85

Thuy, Xuan, 3–6, 64
tourism in Vietnam, 74–75
trade embargo, 74

U
UNICEF, 8
United States Army, 26–30, 31–33

V
vengeance, avoidance of, 32
Vietnam
    attempts to end, 1–3, 3–6
    Cambodia and, 56–60, 67–68
    as election issue, 47
    involvement in, 45–46
    legacy of war in, 74–75
    meetings with Xuan Thuy and, 3–6, 64
    military setbacks in, 70–71
    negotiations with Le Duc Tho and, 65–67, 71–73, 74–75, 76
    Nobel Peace Prize and, 6–10
    policy for, 53
    Soviet Union and, 70–71
    withdrawal from, 62–63
Vietnam Special Studies Group, 60
Vietnamization, 62–65, 70
völkerball, 15–16

W
Walters, Vernon, 1, 4
Washington Special Action Group, 60
Watergate, 10, 60, 79–81, 85, 87–89
Wilson, Woodrow, 55
wiretaps, 59–60, 78, 87
A World Restored, 35, 36–39
World War II, involvement in, 26–30
Würzburg, 17

X
Xuan Thuy. See Thuy, Xuan

Y
Yankee Stadium, 24

HEATHER LEHR WAGNER is a writer and editor. She is the author of more than 30 books exploring social and political issues and focusing on the lives of prominent men and women. She earned a B.A. in political science from Duke University, and an M.A. in government from the College of William and Mary. She lives with her husband and family in Pennsylvania. She is also the author of *Elie Wiesel* in the MODERN PEACEMAKERS series.